TEXAS WILDLIFE VIEWING GUIDE

Gary L. Graham

FALCON PRESS®

ACKNOWLEDGMENTS

Primary funding for the research and development of this book was provided by: Texas Parks and Wildlife Department, The Favrot Fund, National Fish and Wildlife Foundation, The Brown Foundation, USDA Forest Service, Texas General Land Office, U.S. Fish and Wildlife Service, The McAshan Educational and Charitable Trust, Lower Colorado River Authority, National Park Service, and the U.S. Bureau of Land Management. Other important contributors include the Fanwood Foundation, the U.S. Bureau of Reclamation, and the Texas Nature Conservancy.

Andrew Sansom, Executive Director of the Texas Parks and Wildlife Department, in his strong commitment to the Wildlife Viewing Project, provided partial funding and an office for the project manager. Garry Mauro, Commissioner of the Texas General Land Office, was also an early and strong supporter of the project.

The Texas Wildlife Viewing Guide Committee was composed of Gary Graham, Project Manager on contract with Defenders of Wildlife; Laird Fowler, Catrina Martin, and George Zappler, Texas Parks and Wildlife Department; Larry Bonner and Jim Morphew, USDA Forest Service; Jon Andrew, Jim Clark, and Deborah Holle, U.S. Fish and Wildlife Service; Jennifer Thompson, Texas General Land Office; Geoffrey Smith, National Park Service; Kirk Cowan, Lower Colorado River Authority; Stephen Helfert, U.S. Bureau of Reclamation; Jeff Weigel, Texas Nature Conservancy; Jane Lyons, National Audubon Society; and Carey Weber, U.S. Army Corps of Engineers. These people were instrumental in nominating sites and reviewing the manuscript.

Kate Davies and Sara Vickerman, Defenders of Wildlife, provided guidance throughout the development of this guide. Jim Cole, USDA Forest Service, was helpful during the early phase of the project. Bobby Alexander, Brent Ortego, David Riskind, and Charles Winkler, Texas Parks and Wildlife Department, frequently provided information and assistance. Many other individuals nominated viewing sites and provided support materials. The artist for the biodiversity section, Linda Wells of the Texas Parks and Wildlife Department, was particularly helpful and patient.

This book is dedicated to the biologists, wildlife managers, and educators who work to provide quality wildlife viewing and educational opportunities to the public while protecting wildlife populations and their habitats.

Author and State Project Manager:
Gary L. Graham

National Watchable Wildlife Program Coordinator:
Kate Davies, Defenders of Wildlife

Maps:
Alex Tait

Front Cover Photo: Oscelot ERWIN AND PEGGY BAUER
Back Cover Photos: Davis Mountains State Park RALPH LEE HOPKINS
Sennett's white-tailed hawk with young LARRY R. DITTO

CONTENTS

PROJECT SPONSORS

The TEXAS PARKS AND WILDLIFE DEPARTMENT strives to preserve, conserve and protect the State's unequaled natural and cultural resources, and to maximize the public's opportunity to enjoy them. In recognition of the increasing public interest in wildlife watching, the department is pleased to sponsor this program. The Texas Conservation Passport, available for $25, provides numerous benefits to the holder and generates funds to help achieve our conservation goals. Texas Parks and Wildlife Department, 4200 Smith School Road, Austin, TX, 78744. (512) 389-4800.

DEFENDERS OF WILDLIFE is a national, nonprofit organization of more than 80,000 members and supporters dedicated to preserving the natural abundance and diversity of wildlife and its habitat. A one-year membership is $20 and includes six issues of the bimonthly magazine. To join or for further information, write or call Defenders of Wildlife, 1244 Nineteenth St., NW, Washington, DC 20036. (202) 659-9510.

The FOREST SERVICE, U.S. DEPARTMENT OF AGRICUL-TURE, has a mandate to protect, improve, and wisely use the nation's forest and range resources for multiple purposes to benefit all Americans. The national forests and grasslands of Texas are sponsors of this program to promote awareness and enjoyment of fish and wildlife on our national forest lands. USDA Forest Service, 701 N. First St., Lufkin, Texas 75901. (409) 639-8501.

 The constitutional responsibility of the TEXAS GENERAL LAND OFFICE is to make money for the state through the use of state-owned lands. The land office has added to this charge the moral responsibility of protecting and preserving the environment of those lands. This includes coastal management, oil spill prevention and response, beach cleanups, and work on international agreements to ban dumping in the Gulf. Texas General Land Office, 1700 North Congress Avenue, Austin, TX, 78701-1495. (512) 463-5001.

 The U.S. FISH AND WILDLIFE SERVICE is pleased to support the Watchable Wildlife effort in furtherance of its mission to preserve, protect, and enhance fish and wildlife resources and their habitats for use and enjoyment by the American public. U.S. Fish and Wildlife Service, 500 Gold Ave., SW, P.O. Box 1306, Albuquerque, NM 87103. (505) 766-2321

 The TEXAS DEPARTMENT OF TRANSPORTATION manages a network of 77,000 highway miles serving millions of citizens and visitors. Environmental protection is a priority throughout the transit system. The Department also operates the Travel Information Centers and produces free travel-tourism literature, including the *Texas State Travel Guide* and the official highway map. TxDOT, 125 E. 11th Street, Austin, TX 78701-2483, (512) 463-8601.

 The LOWER COLORADO RIVER AUTHORITY owns and manages over 25,000 acres of public land located along a chain of five highland lakes and the Colorado River. Developed parks, primitive recreation areas, and the Colorado River Trail offer ample opportunities for wildlife viewing. LCRA, P.O. Box 220, Austin, TX, 78767-0220. (512) 473-3200.

 The NATIONAL PARK SERVICE, which conserves park areas and "leaves them unimpaired for the enjoyment of present and future generations," protects biodiversity by preserving critical wildlife habitat. In Texas, lands managed by the NPS include many of the wonderfully diverse habitats found here, from grasslands and forests to desert mountains and gulf seashores. NPS, P.O. Box 728, Santa Fe, New Mexico 87504-0728, (505) 988-6375.

 The BUREAU OF LAND MANAGEMENT is responsible for the balanced management of the public lands and resources and their various values so that they are considered in a combination that will best serve the needs of the American people. Management is based upon the principles of multiple use and sustained yield, in a combination of uses that takes into account the long-term needs of future generations for renewable and nonrenewable resources. BLM, 221 North Service Rd., Moore, OK, 73160-4946. (405) 794-9624.

 THE NATIONAL FISH AND WILDLIFE FOUNDATION, chartered by Congress to stimulate private giving to conservation, is an independent not-for-profit organization. Using federally funded challenge grants, it forges partnerships between the public and private sectors to conserve the nation's fish, wildlife, and plants. National Fish and Wildlife Foundation, 18th and C Street N.W., Washington, DC 20240, (202) 208-4051.

As Governor of Texas, it is with great pleasure that I invite you to discover and enjoy one of our state's most valuable assets—our incredible wildlife.

The diversity and abundance of wildlife in Texas is astounding. You can start by watching antelope fawns running after their mother in the national grasslands of the Panhandle, or by looking for Mexican birds in the semi-tropical woodlands of the Rio Grande Valley. Visit the eastern pineywoods, where the endangered red-cockaded woodpecker can be viewed, or hike through the newly created Big Bend Ranch State Natural Area, rich with western wildlife. Or perhaps you would rather start in the Central Texas Hill Country, where white-tailed deer abound and where you can witness the flight of almost a million bats from beneath the Congress Avenue Bridge in Austin.

No matter where you start, you'll be amazed by the wildlife viewing and photographic opportunities awaiting you in Texas. This book will help you plan trips and learn more about the animals and their habitats.

So bring along your binoculars, plenty of film for your camera,

 and a Texas Conservation Passport, then head out to one of the 142 sites identified in this book. We're proud to offer some of the finest wildlife viewing in the world.

Sincerely,

Ann Richards
Governor

INTRODUCTION

Everybody can enjoy watching wildlife, in part because there are so many ways to do it. You can observe wildlife alone, with your family, or as part of an organized group. Watch the antics of songbirds and squirrels from your window or wait quietly in a remote blind to glimpse a bobcat scouting for mice. At night, you can drive through the Franklin Mountains and hope to see a fox, or sit quietly by a desert pond listening to the eerie trill of hundreds of toads. You can even enjoy wildlife when it can't be seen by walking through the pineywoods on a winter morning and listening for the nasal, hornlike call of a red-breasted nuthatch or the hammering of a red-cockaded woodpecker. Following javelina tracks in the mud from yesterday's rain or dinosaur tracks made millions of years ago can teach you about animal behavior. And even the most sober among us will thrill to the spectacle of the sudden autumn arrival of thousands of ducks and cranes at a playa lake, or the sunset flight of a million bats leaving their cave for a night's feeding.

Whatever your methods or interests, watching wildlife is fun and fast becoming one of the most popular American pastimes. Such intense public interest, however, can lead to problems unless viewers exercise courtesy and common sense. Learn respect for animals and their habitats, know the regulations, and show consideration for private property and regard for the activities of others. Consider the following suggestions:

VIEWING TIPS

• The first and last hours of daylight are generally the best times to view or photograph most species, but explore a variety of times, including after dark.
• Quick movements and loud noises will normally scare wildlife. Whisper when you speak, and be as quiet as possible. Approach streams slowly and use vegetation as a screen to avoid scaring fish in shallow water. You can also use your car, truck, or boat as a viewing blind.
• Binoculars and field guides will enhance your trip. Use your ears to locate and identify wildlife. You can learn particular bird songs from available cassette sets.
• Patience is important. Give yourself enough time to allow animals to enter or return to an area. It may take persistence and a little luck to see some of the species listed in this guide because they are uncommon or rare. Do not expect to see all of the described wildlife during each outing.
• Be sure to bring insect repellent when visiting sites where mosquitoes are likely, such as many of the coastal and eastern sites.
• Keep far enough away from nests and dens to avoid disturbing breeding wildlife, which are especially sensitive. Never chase or flush wildlife. Wildlife watching on beaches offers special challenges because many birds, some threatened, nest exposed on the sand. Do not drive or walk in these areas.
• Honor the rights of private landowners. Gain permission from private landowners before entering their property.

• Always maintain a safe distance between yourself and rattlesnakes, alligators, mountain lions, and bears. Phone a TPWD conservation officer if you suspect an animal is sick or orphaned. Remember that in many cases, young animals that appear to be alone have not been abandoned; allow them to find their own way.

• Leave wildlife habitat in better condition than you found it. Pick up trash.

THE NATIONAL WATCHABLE WILDLIFE PROGRAM

Texas, already internationally known for its spectacular wildlife viewing , is entering a new and exciting era with respect to wildlife conservation. Historically, state wildlife programs were funded through license fees for hunting and fishing and federal taxes on the equipment used—guns, ammunition, and fishing tackle. These funds were used to enhance and preserve wildlife habitat, benefitting game and nongame species alike. But participation in hunting has gradually declined, while the number of adults involved in wildlife watching and related activities has increased tremendously. Consequently, the challenge faced by wildlife agencies in the 1990s is to develop new conservation programs and funding strategies that serve the entire public while guaranteeing abundant wildlife to watch into the next century and beyond.

In response to this situation, federal and state land and wildlife management agencies in Texas have formed a partnership with conservation organizations. This effort, known as the Texas Wildlife Viewing Project, is part of the National Watchable Wildlife Program, a partnership coordinated by Defenders of Wildlife. The goal of this initiative is to provide citizens of Texas, as well as visitors, a new opportunity to enjoy and better appreciate the wildlife of this incredible state. The *Texas Wildlife Viewing Guide* is an important step in this effort and will serve as a focal point for the project for years to come.

In the field, individual sites are being enhanced through interpretive signing, trail driving-tour development, and construction of viewing blinds or platforms. Further, the state is opening wildlife management areas to wildlife viewing and acquiring habitat to protect many nongame species. To fund these initiatives, user fees will be initiated or increased, and new programs promoted, including the Nongame and Endangered Species Conservation Fund and the Texas Conservation Passport.

The success of these programs depends upon your active involvement. Use this guide to observe, photograph, and learn more about wildlife species so that you can effectively participate in their conservation. Use it to plan trips to one or many specific sites, or to augment a trip taken for another purpose. Support wildlife conservation agency efforts to fund wildlife diversity programs and support local economies where possible. Above all, relish the wildlife discoveries you make and the memories you create.

HOW TO USE THIS GUIDE

This guide is organized by the ten ecological regions of the state, with each viewing site described in the appropriate region. Each site description includes the featured wildlife species or groups (displayed with symbols at the beginning of each description), information about viewing probability (high to low), and viewing season. Specific directions are given to each site and may include some of the following abbreviations:

FM and RR—Farm to Market and Ranch Roads.

PR—Park Roads.

The name of the owner or manager of each site is given, plus a telephone number where additional site information can be obtained. Available facilities and recreational opportunities are symbolized at the end of each description.

FEATURED WILDLIFE

 Songbirds Perching Birds

 Waterfowl

 Upland Birds

 Wading Birds

 Shorebirds

 Marine Birds

 Birds of Prey

 Hoofed Mammals

 Carnivores Mammals

 Small Mammals

 Reptiles Amphibians

 Freshwater Mammals

 Seals, Sea Lions, Sea Otters

Whales Dolphins

 Fish

Tidepools

Bats

Insects

 Wildflowers

FACILITIES AND RECREATION

P Parking   **$** Entry Fee   Restrooms   Handicapped Accessible   Picnic   Restaurant   Lodging

Camping   Hiking   Cross-country Skiing   Bicycling   Boat Ramp   Large Boats   Small Boats

SITE OWNER/MANAGER ABBREVIATIONS

ACOE   U.S. Army Corps of Engineers
GLO   Texas General Land Office
NPS   National Park Service
PVT   Private ownership
TPWD   Texas Parks and Wildlife Department
USFS   U.S. Forest Service
USFWS   U.S. Fish and Wildlife Service

MAP INFORMATION

Texas is divided into ten travel regions shown on this map. Wildlife viewing sites in this guide are numbered consecutively in a general pattern. Each region forms a seperate section in this book, and each section begins with a map of that region.

1 This symbol indicates the location and number of a wildlife viewing site.

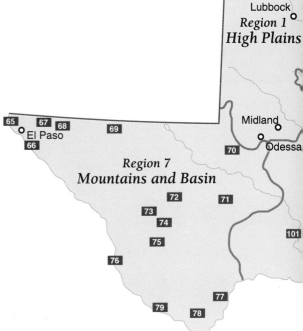

As you travel across Texas, look for these special highway signs that identify wildlife viewing sites. The binoculars logo and directional arrow will help guide you to the viewing area.

NOTE: It is very important to read the directions provided in each site description—highway signs may refer to more than one site along a particular route.

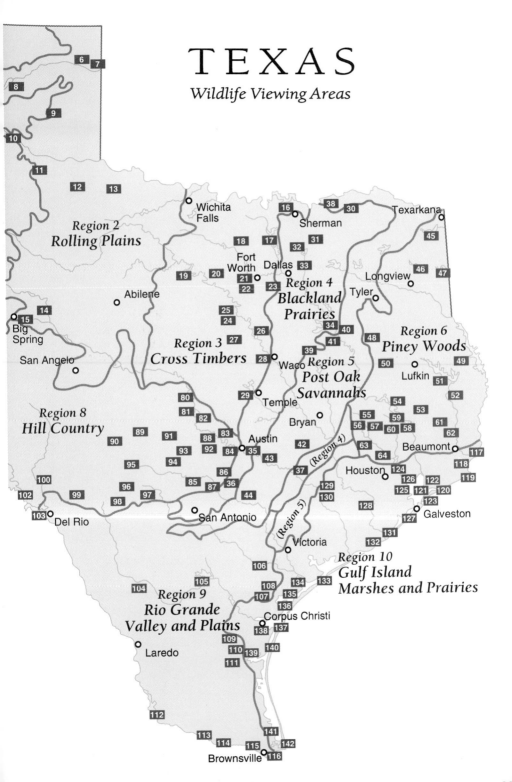

TEXAS
Wildlife Viewing Areas

6 7

8

9

10

11

12   13

Wichita
Falls   16   38   30   Texarkana

Region 2   Sherman
Rolling Plains   45

18   17   31
Fort   32
Worth   Dallas   33
19   20   21   *Region 4*   Longview   46   47
22   23   **Blackland**   Tyler
Abilene   **Prairies**

25   *Region 6*
24   26   34   40   48   **Piney Woods**
14   41
15   *Region 3*   27   39   50   49
Big   **Cross Timbers**   28   Waco   *Region 5*   Lufkin
Spring   **Post Oak**   51
San Angelo   **Savannahs**   52
80   54
81   29   Temple   55   59   53
Region 8   82   Bryan   56   57   60   58   61
Hill Country   89   91   88   83   63   62
90   93   92   84   35   42   64   Beaumont   117
95   94   43   37   (*Region 4*)   118
100   86   *Region 5*   124   119
102   99   96   85   87   36   129   126   122
103   Del Rio   98   97   44   130   128   125   121   120
                                                            123
San Antonio   127   Galveston

(*Region 5*)   131
Victoria   132

106   *Region 10*
105   **Gulf Island**
104   *Region 9*   108   134   133   **Marshes and Prairies**
Rio Grande   107   135
Valley and Plains   136
Corpus Christi
138   137
109
Laredo   110   139   140
111

112

113
114   115   141
Brownsville   116   142

13

Mammal Species
168 - total native
10 - specialties
6 - disappeared

Bird Species
590 - total native
49 - specialties
6 - disappeared

SPECIES: Whether it has a great many species or only a few, each area of the earth is unique with respect to biodiversity, meaning the variety of animals, plants, habitats, and ecosystems. With almost 1,200 species, Texas has more native species of vertebrates, animals with backbones, than any other state. Texas also has the greatest diversity of birds in the United States, but far less than Peru in South America, which has over 1,700 species. Two of the wildlife viewing sites in this guide, Aranasas and Laguna Atascosa National Wildlife Refuges, have recorded about 390 kinds of birds, more than any of the other national refuges.

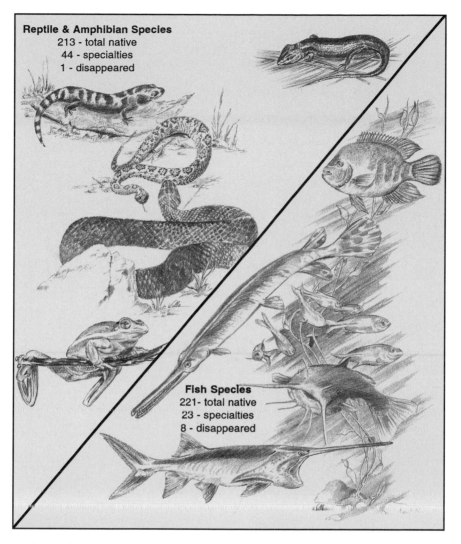

Reptile & Amphibian Species
213 - total native
44 - specialties
1 - disappeared

Fish Species
221 - total native
23 - specialties
8 - disappeared

With 32 of the 42 species known from the United States, Texas also has more kinds of bats than any state. Fungi, bacteria, and other animals, such as worms and insects, also are important components of biodiversity. Big Bend National Park, known for its diversity of wildlife, has over 1,200 species of butterflies and moths. The greatest diversity within Texas is found in the mountainous west or the subtropical south, where many Texas specialties, species not found in any other state north of Mexico, reach the northern limits of their distribution. What Is Texas Biodiversity? Incredible!

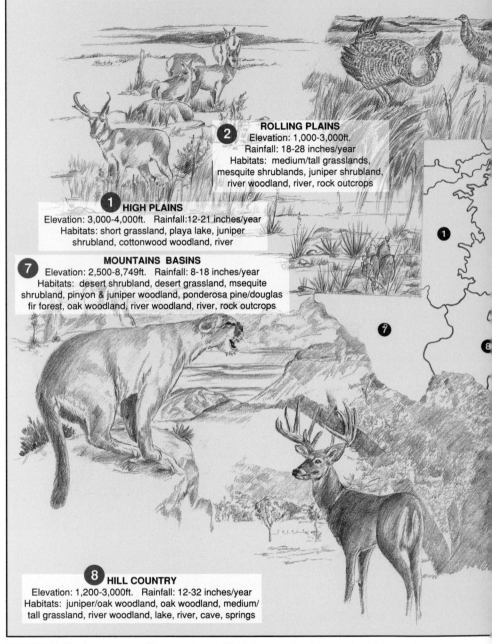

2 ROLLING PLAINS
Elevation: 1,000-3,000ft.
Rainfall: 18-28 inches/year
Habitats: medium/tall grasslands,
mesquite shrublands, juniper shrubland,
river woodland, river, rock outcrops

1 HIGH PLAINS
Elevation: 3,000-4,000ft.   Rainfall:12-21 inches/year
Habitats: short grassland, playa lake, juniper
shrubland, cottonwood woodland, river

7 MOUNTAINS BASINS
Elevation: 2,500-8,749ft.   Rainfall: 8-18 inches/year
Habitats: desert shrubland, desert grassland, msequite
shrubland, pinyon & juniper woodland, ponderosa pine/douglas
fir forest, oak woodland, river woodland, river, rock outcrops

8 HILL COUNTRY
Elevation: 1,200-3,000ft.   Rainfall: 12-32 inches/year
Habitats: juniper/oak woodland, oak woodland, medium/
tall grassland, river woodland, lake, river, cave, springs

HABITATS: An outstanding variety of habitats, which are the places where animals live, is one of the important reasons why Texas has such high biodiversity. There are 10 distinct ecological regions and each region has a variety of habitats within it. The geographic location of Texas contributes to this habitat diversity in that eastern habitats meet western ones and southern subtropical habitats meet northern temperate ones. A large area of land will usually have a great deal of variation in climate and landscapes, factors influencing habitat diversity.

BLACKLAND PRAIRES
4
Elevation: 250-700ft.
Rainfall: 30-45 inches/year
Habitats: tall grassland, river woodland, lake, river

POST OAK SAVANNAHS
5
Elevation: 200-500 ft.
Rainfall: 30-45 inches/year
Habitats: oak woodland, tall grassland, bottomland hardwood forest, lake, river, bogs

CROSS TIMBERS & PRAIRIES
Elevation: 500-1,500ft.
Rainfall: 28-35 inches/year
Habitats: oak woodland, tall grassland, lake, river woodland, river

PINEYWOODS
6
Elevation: 200-700 ft.
Rainfall: 40-56 inches/year
Habitats: pine/oak forest, bottomland hardwood forest, longleaf pine woodland, beach/magnolia forest, lake, river bogs

LOWER RIO GRANDE VALLEY & PLAINS
9
Elevation: sea level - 1,000ft.
Rainfall : 18-30 inches/year
Habitats: mesquite woodland, woody shrubland, river, subtropical forest, palm forests

GULF ISLANDS, MARSHES, & PRAIRIES
10
Elevation: sea level - 250ft.
Rainfall : 28-59 inches/year
Habitats: fresh/saltwater marshes, hardwood forest, live oak woodland, tall grassland, sandy dunes, sandy beach, mud flat, bay, open gulf

Texas is big! Covering 266,807 square miles, 15 of the 50 states could fit within its borders. Winters are severe in the northern Panhandle, but very mild in the extreme south where habitats are more tropical. Annual rainfall varies from 8 inches in deserts of the west to almost 60 inches along the Sabine River in the east. The state has 91 mountains that are a mile or more high. The highest is in the Guadalupe National Park, one of the viewing sites, and is 2,000 feet higher than the highest mountain east of the Mississippi River. Texas also has a greater volume of inland water than any state except Alaska.

17

WENDY SHATTIL/BOB ROZINSKI

GARY L. GRAHAM

PAUL SHIPPINDALE AND DAVID HILLIS

JEFF FOOTT

CONNECTIONS: The wildlife we view, and the habitats where they live are parts of ecosystems where animals and plants interact with each other, the soil, water, air, and in some places, fire. Certain fishes and salamanders, including several endangered species, live in springs that drain aquifers, which are underground bodies of water that depend on distant rainfall. Through a complex web of connections, much of the familiar coastal wildlife relies on fresh water and nutrients delivered to estuaries and bays by rivers resulting from inland rain. Historically, grasslands were disturbed by fire and grazing activities of bison and prairie dogs, which helped maintain the grassland by discouraging the

WHAT IN THE WORLD IS IT?

JOHN SNYDER

JOHN SNYDER

NATIONAL WILDFLOWER RESEARCH CENTER

the growth of shrubs and trees. Periodic ground fires prevent young pine trees from becoming too dense and promote biodiversity by encouraging the growth of plants used as food by browsing and seed-eating animals. The presence of red-cockaded woodpeckers is connected to open forest with old pine trees that have heart disease, a condition that allows nest holes to be bored inside live trees. Texas is connected to the tropics through many of our songbirds, which migrate north from Latin America to breed here, adding to our biodiversity and viewing pleasure.

LAURENCE PARENT

LAURENCE PARENT

LAURENCE PARENT

PEOPLE: The actions of people can cause the loss, maintenance, or restoration of biodiverstiy. When people disrupt ecosystems, some habitats are lost and certain wildlife disappear. Using ground water faster than it is replenished can lead to the death of spring ecosystems. Urbanization, conversion of grasslands and forests to pastures and croplands, and the flooding of bottomland hardwoods to form lakes cause large-scale losses of habitats and biodiversity. More and more people, however, are becoming aware of these issues and are contributing to the solutions.

ROSE FARMER/NATIONAL AUDUBON SOCIETY

JOHN SNYDER

GRADY ALLEN

Public involvement is needed for conservation success. What can you do? Start by planting native shrubs and flowers that attract additional wildlife to your yard, neighborhood, or ranch. Volunteer to help with larger habitat restoration projects. Get involved in the political process by communicating with local, state, or national politicians. Question activities that could reduce biodiversity and support governmental actions to promote wildlife and their habitats. Become informed and effective by join conservation organizations. Invite friends and relatives to watch wildlife and help them appreciate the remarkable biodiversity of Texas.

Photo, next page: Cattle Egret GRADY ALLEN

REGION 1: HIGH PLAINS

These flat, featureless plains were once carpeted with short grasses such as blue grama and buffalo grass. Immense herds of buffalo and pronghorn antelope thundered across vast prairie dog towns. Now the plains are mostly irrigated croplands and the native vegetation includes more mesquite and junipers. Elevation ranges from 3,000 to 4,000 feet; rainfall varies from twelve to twenty-one inches per year.

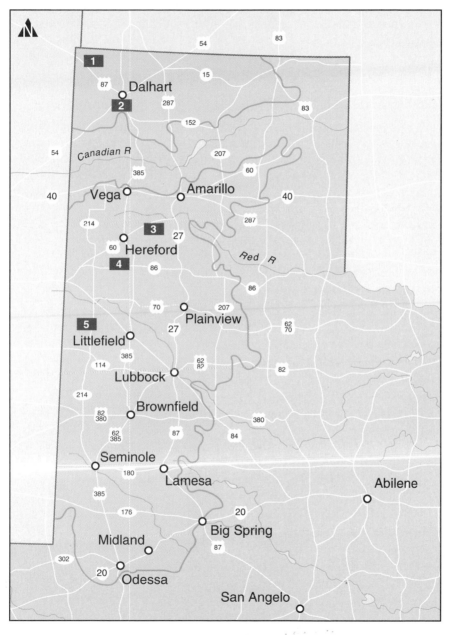

1	Rita Blanca National Grassland	4	Playa Lakes Driving Tour
2	Lake Rita Blanca	5	Muleshoe National Wildlife
3	Buffalo Lake National Wildlife Refuge		Refuge

1 RITA BLANCA NATIONAL GRASSLAND

Description: Pronghorn antelope, red and swift fox, coyote, prairie dog, raptors, and grassland birds are characteristic of this site. Birds that nest here and are more difficult to view in other parts of Texas include long-billed curlew, ferruginous and Swainson's hawks, ring-necked pheasant, mountain plover, and lark bunting. Sandhill cranes are present in the fall. Scattered ponds attract waterfowl and other wildlife. The gently rolling grassland, rich with native wildflowers, is managed for recreation, grassland agriculture, and wildlife.

Viewing information: Burrowing owl and ferruginous hawk are viewed near prairie dog towns such as near the intersection of Farm Road 296 and Farm Road 1879. Thompson Grove Recreation Site, also near the intersection, contains some of the only trees in the area and offers excellent birding. Viewing probability is high for pronghorn antelope and moderate for coyote and foxes all year; wildflowers and songbirds are most common in late spring and early summer. A network of unimproved roads provides good hiking, biking, and wildlife watching trails. The grassland is divided into over thirty-five separate units surrounded by private land. Maps available at headquarters will help you locate water sources and avoid trespassing. Unimproved roads can become a problem following heavy rain or snow. To avoid disturbance, wildlife at ponds should be viewed from a distance during the nesting season.

Directions: *From Texline near the New Mexico border, drive east for about fourteen miles on Texas 296 to where the road turns sharply north. Either follow 296 north to the grassland west of Thompson Grove or continue east on the unimproved county road for a scenic drive through the core of the grasslands.*

Ownership: USFS (806-362-4254)
Size: 77,463 acres **Closest Town:** Texline

Black-tailed prairie dogs, named for their bark-like calls, are enjoyable to watch and important to the ecology of grasslands. Unrelated to domestic dogs, these rodents were so numerous at the turn of the century that one biologist described a prairie dog town 250 miles long.
SHERM SPOELSTRA

2 | LAKE RITA BLANCA

Description: Spectacular flocks of geese and ducks roost here during migration and through the winter. Mule deer, swift and red fox, coyotes, skunks, raccoons, scaled quail, several species of hawks, and songbirds occupy surrounding grasslands and canyons. Shorebirds are numerous during migration.

Viewing information: Viewing probability is high for waterfowl, quail, and songbirds; moderate for other wildlife. Bald eagles are occasionally observed during winter.

Directions: Go south from Dalhart on FM 281 for 1.5 miles to entrance.

Ownership: Dallam and Hartley Counties (TPWD, 806-353-0486)
Size: 1,924 acres
Closest Town: Dalhart

3 | BUFFALO LAKE NATIONAL WILDLIFE REFUGE

Description: Instead of a lake or buffalo, which are no longer present, visitors find a surprising diversity of wildlife viewing opportunities here. Common nighthawks, songbirds, great horned owls, and porcupines are viewed on the Cottonwood Canyon Birding Trail where pheasants and bobwhite also call. Interactions of prairie dogs, burrowing owls, and ferruginous hawks can be observed along the Prairie Dog Town Interpretive Walking Trail. Bobcats, coyotes, mule deer, porcupines, badgers, and owls can be seen from a five-mile auto tour featuring useful interpretive signs. An observation deck overlooking a marsh provides a chance to view waterfowl during winter, if there is water.

Viewing Information: While driving just before, after, or during the night, viewing probability is low for carnivores and porcupines but moderate to high for deer. Viewing for nighthawks and songbirds is best during the spring and summer. Prairie dog and burrowing owl viewing is always good. Ferruginous hawks and bald and golden eagles are uncommon during the winter.

Directions: From Interstate 40 in Amarillo, go south fourteen miles on Interstate 27 to U.S. 60. Go south two miles, then west ten miles on U.S. 60 to Umbarger and 1.5 miles south on FM 168 to entrance.

Ownership: USFWS (806-499-3382)
Size: 7,664 acres **Closest Town:** Umbarger

 **PLAYA LAKES DRIVING TOUR**

Description: Hundreds of thousands of ducks, geese, cranes, and shorebirds use playa lakes during the fall, winter, and spring. Frogs and toads also can be abundant at these lakes. Coyotes, striped skunks, ring-necked pheasants, grassland songbirds, and reptiles are observed in surrounding prairies. Hawks, eagles, and osprey are occasionally seen.

Viewing Information: Scan the playa lakes, fields, and feedlots from public roads on a driving loop from Dimmitt. Most of the area is private land where public entry is not allowed. Visitors can hike to view wildlife at the Dimmitt Unit, about five miles west of Dimmitt. Look for TPWD signs marking property boundary. Avoid dirt roads during wet periods. No facilities at this site.

Directions: From the junction of U.S. 385 and FM 2392, drive west on 2392 4.3 miles, turn south on dirt road for .5 mile to Dimmitt Unit. Return to 2392 and go west 1.6 miles, turn south on FM 1055 for 2.7 miles to Texas 86. Drive west four miles on 86, then south on FM 1524 for two miles. Drive west on dirt road for one mile, then south .4 mile to Armstrong Playa. Continue south .6 mile, and east one mile, then south and east on FM 1524 for 14.2 miles to U.S. 385. Drive 9.4 miles north on 385 to end in Dimmitt.

Ownership: Various (806-353-0486, TPWD)
Size: 42.1 miles **Closest Town:** Dimmitt

To witness and hear hundreds of nearby snow geese is one of nature's most moving experiences. Snow geese can be recognized in flight by the wavy, irregular shape of their formations, unlike the well-defined V of Canada geese. The species also includes a darker color phase, the "blue" goose. ART WOLFE

Description: One of the largest concentrations of lesser sandhill cranes in North America—often more than 100,000 birds at one time—winters at this grassland refuge. Thousands of ducks and geese use the refuge during the winter months. Shorebirds and a large diversity of songbirds migrate through the area. Golden eagles are common during the fall and winter. Porcupines, badgers, coyotes, and bobcats are occasionally seen from the refuge roads.

Viewing Information: Cranes arrive by the first of October, become most abundant from December to mid-February, and leave near the end of March. They are best observed during early morning or late afternoon as they leave or enter the playa lakes where they roost. Spring and fall are the best times to watch shorebirds near playas and songbirds in trees near the headquarters.

Directions: Take Texas 114 west from Lubbock for about fifty-five miles to Morton, then twenty miles north on Texas 214 to entrance.

Ownership: USFWS (806-946-3341)
Size: 5,809 acres **Closest Town:** Muleshoe

The Texas population of sandhill cranes is the largest concentration of any species of crane in the world. Wetlands are vital habitat for these birds, as they prefer to roost in shallow water for protection against predators.

STEVE BENTSEN

REGION 2: ROLLING PLAINS

Several Texas rivers begin in these gently rolling hills and broad flats. Rivers have cut canyons that shelter some plants and animals typical of the Rocky Mountains. Native prairies, once a sweeping expanse of sideoats grama, little bluestem, and other grasses, are now largely replaced by cultivated fields and livestock pastures. Elevation ranges from 1,000 to 3,000 feet; annual rainfall varies from eighteen to twenty-eight inches.

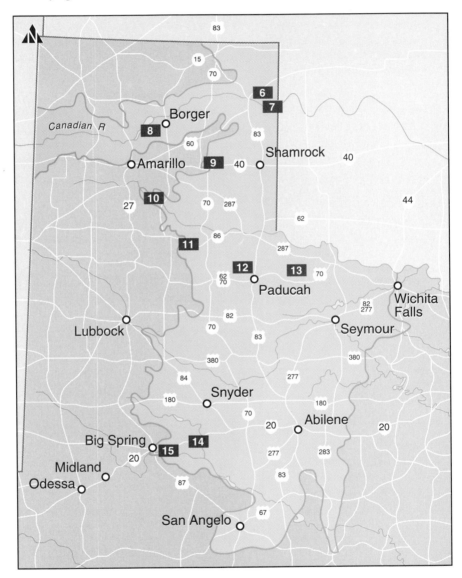

6	Gene Howe Wildlife Management Area	11	Caprock Canyons State Park
7	Lake Marvin	12	Matador Wildlife Management Area
8	Lake Meredith National Recreation Area	13	Copper Breaks State Park
9	Lake McClellan/McClellan Creek National Grassland	14	Lake Colorado City State Park
10	Palo Duro Canyon State Park	15	Big Spring State Park

Description: This site features wild turkey, bobwhite quail, lesser prairie chickens, pheasants, bobcats, white-tailed deer, beaver, and small mammals. The major habitats are arid, sandy hills covered with sagebrush and grass bordering the floodplain with its tall cottonwood groves, scattered smaller trees, large meadows and the Canadian River. Mississippi kites soar overhead from late spring into fall. Fall colors are particularly beautiful.

Viewing Information: Viewing probability for most wildlife is moderate to high. Although difficult to find most of the year, the booming courtship calls of male prairie chickens can be heard near prairie dog towns in the spring. The birds are easily disturbed during this season, so please view from at least 100 yards away. Most wildlife can be viewed from FM 2266 or the numerous dirt roads, which should not be driven following heavy rains. Ducks and shorebirds can be viewed on the river during migration. Wildlife viewing may be discouraged during hunting seasons. A Texas Conservation Passport and registration at headquarters are required for entry.

Directions: *Turn east on FM 2266 just north of the U.S. 60/83 bridge over the Canadian River and go six miles to the area headquarters, where a map can be obtained.*

Ownership: TPWD (806-323-8642)
Size: 5,821 acres **Closest Town:** Canadian

Texas has six species of native cats, more than any other state. The bobcat, a supreme rodent catcher, is by far the most common, occuring from border to border. STEVE BENTSEN

7 LAKE MARVIN

Description: This pretty lake surrounded by cottonwoods and grasslands is home to wood duck, migratory waterfowl, Mississippi kite, red-headed woodpecker, wild turkey, songbirds, bobcat, small mammals, and white-tailed deer. A wildlife trail and observation platform along the edge of the lake provides exceptional viewing of marsh species, including turtles, fish, and an occasional muskrat or beaver.

Viewing information: Probability of viewing wood ducks is high and the fortunate visitor may watch one fly from the "Big Tree," an old cottonwood that is now a historical landmark. Most species can be easily viewed all year from the road circling the lake or the trails. Waterfowl are most abundant during winter. Bobcat tracks and beaver signs are common though the animals themselves are rare. Yellow cottonwoods brighten the area during the fall.

Directions: *Turn east on FM 2266 just north of the U.S. 60/83 bridge over the Canadian River and go eleven miles to lake.*

Ownership: USFS (405-497-2143)
Size: 575 acres
Closest Town: Canadian

Ring-necked pheasants, although beautiful and common in places, are not a native species—they were brought to the United States from Asia in the early 1930s. Ten more species of birds, including house sparrows and starlings, and twelve mammals, including nutria and red fox, have been introduced to Texas.

BRENT PARRETT/N.E. STOCK PHOTO

8 LAKE MEREDITH NATIONAL RECREATION AREA

Description: Sparkling blue waters and colorful canyons of Lake Meredith contrast with the arid, flat Llano Estacado, as the surrounding high plains are called. Waterfowl are scattered over the lake; numerous raptors, including golden eagles and up to forty bald eagles at one time, fly overhead. Diverse songbirds, white-tailed deer, and small mammals occupy the canyon woodlands, and pronghorn antelope and mule deer frequent the grasslands. Beaver and rails are occasionally seen in the marshes behind the dam.

Viewing information: Viewing probabilities are best for waterfowl and bald eagles during winter. Wild turkey, northern flickers, horned larks, and rufous-crowned sparrows are permanent residents; red-headed woodpeckers and Cassin's sparrows are summer residents. Mountain and eastern bluebirds, Townsend's solitaire, and American tree sparrows are present only in winter. Porcupines, skunks, raccoons, and rabbits are easily observed, whereas ring-tails, badgers, and bobcats are more difficult. Lake Meredith Aquatic and Wildlife Museum is in Fritch.

Directions: Drive north from Amarillo on Texas 136 for about thirty-five miles to NPS headquarters in Fritch where detailed maps can be obtained.

Ownership: NPS/BREC (NPS, 806-857-3151)
Size: 45,000 acres
Closest Town: Fritch

9 LAKE MCCLELLAN AND MCCLELLAN CREEK NATIONAL GRASSLAND

Description: Grassland species such as dickcissel and pronghorn antelope, geese, wild turkey and pheasant, white-tailed deer and bobcats make this an interesting viewing site. Lizards are abundant and snakes are common during the summer. Bald eagles are frequently observed during the winter.

Viewing information: Pronghorn antelope are rare, but wild turkey, bob-white, and white-tailed deer are abundant. Viewing probability for bobcat is low. Grassland birds are most diverse during the spring and fall migrations, but sparrows are most easily seen during the winter.

Directions: East from Amarillo on Interstate 40 about fifty-five miles to FM 2477. Drive north three miles to lake.

Ownership: USFS (405-497-2143) **Size:** 1,449 acres **Closest Town:** Alanreed

10 PALO DURO CANYON STATE PARK

Description: Spectacular scenery, reminiscent of the Grand Canyon, startles the visitor driving from the flat plains down to Prairie Dog Town Fork of the Red River. This peaceful stream, which roars following a heavy rain, has carved through recent rocks at the top down to the red Permian shales that are about 250 million years old. Today, permanent residents include mountain lions, bobcats, coyotes, mule deer, porcupines, ringtails, beaver, rabbits, raptors, wild turkey, scaled quail, blue and scrub jays, canyon and rock wrens, and bushtits. Winter brings golden eagles, mountain bluebirds, golden-crowned kinglets, and an occasional northern shrike or evening grosbeak.

Viewing Information: Viewing probability is high for most birds, moderate to high for small mammals, and low for large mammals. Look for tracks and scat along the extensive trail system and banks of the river. Horseback riding is available in the canyon. A visitor center offers excellent exhibits and interpretive materials.

Directions: *South from Amarillo on Interstate 27 to Canyon, then east on Texas 217 for twelve miles to entrance.*

Ownership: TPWD (806-488-2227)
Size: 16,000 acres
Closest Town: Canyon

The Red River canyonlands, in which Palo Duro and Caprock Canyons State Parks are found, include twelve major canyons, more than 125 miles of streams, and cover over 4,000 square miles. Canyons are like inverted mountains: the outstanding visual, geologic, and habitat diversity is below the plains, rather than above. LARRY R. DITTO

CAPROCK CANYONS STATE PARK

Description: Stunning landscapes, sparse vegetation, and diverse wildlife await visitors to this park. River erosion has sculpted rugged canyons from the red rocks, some of which are 250 millions years old. Five plant communities support mule deer, the introduced aoudad sheep, coyotes, bobcats, ringtails, badgers, porcupines, rabbits, and ground squirrels. Each season adds new birds to resident species like great horned owls, golden-fronted woodpeckers, three species of wrens, bushtits, and verdin. Summer brings common poorwills, nesting Swainson's hawks, and painted buntings. Winter additions include mountain bluebirds, numerous sparrows, and waterfowl on Lake Theo.

Viewing Information: Viewing probability for waterfowl and songbirds is high during the winter and spring, respectively, and low to moderate for large mammals and raptors.

Directions: *From Tulia about fifty miles south of Amarillo on Interstate 27, turn east on Texas 86 for fifty-one miles to Quitaque, then north on Farm Road 1065 about three miles to park entrance.*

Ownership: TPWD (806-455-1492)
Size: 13,906 acres **Closest Town:** Quitaque

Mule deer are distinguished from white-tailed deer by their large, mule-like ears, a black-tipped tail, and by antlers (on males) that branch equally, rather than as prongs from a main beam. They occur in drier, open habitats in the Panhandle and far western regions. WYMAN P. MEINZER

12 MATADOR WILDLIFE MANAGEMENT AREA

Description: An excellent site for bobwhite, scaled quail, morning dove, and white-tailed deer. Songbird viewing is particularly good in April and May as migrants pass through the area. Peace River cuts through the rugged rolling plains creating habitat that attracts diverse wildlife, including beaver. Mule deer are occasionally seen.

Viewing Information: Viewing probability is high for featured species, except for beaver, which leaves abundant signs of its nightly activities. This is a large, remote area that requires an off-road vehicle to drive on the network of roads. A Texas Conservation Passport and reservations at the headquarters also are required for entry. Wildlife viewing may be discouraged during the hunting seasons.

Directions: Drive north from Paducah on U.S. 83 about 7.5 miles to FM 3256, then west on 3256 for 3.5 miles to headquarters.

Ownership: TPWD (806-492-3405)
Size: 28,183 acres
Closest Town: Paducah

13 COPPER BREAKS STATE PARK

Description: Scenery, wildlife, history, and interpretation are abundantly represented at this park. Nature, hiking, and equestrian trails pass by lakes, across mesquite-covered mesas, and through beautiful canyons where mule and white-tailed deer, cottontails and jackrabbits, coyotes and bobcats, and raccoons and roadrunners live. Beaver, nutria, and waterfowl are viewed on or near the lakes and ponds. Songbirds are common and migrants are most visible in tall trees around the lake. The visitor center presents exhibits of buffalo and Comanche war chiefs.

Viewing Information: Viewing probability for most species is moderate to high. Mule deer are uncommon and waterfowl are abundant only during the winter migration. Beaver are not often seen because they are active at night.

Directions: From Quanah on U.S. 287, go thirteen miles south on Texas 6 to entrance.

Ownership: TPWD (817-839-4331)
Size: 1,933 acres
Closest Town: Crowell

14 LAKE COLORADO CITY STATE PARK

Description: Gray fox, coyotes, striped skunks, ringtails, raccoons, white-tailed deer, cottontails and jackrabbits, armadillos, ground squirrels, and songbirds occupy habitats surrounding the lake. Waterfowl and wading birds are also seen here.

Viewing Information: Viewing probability for larger carnivores is low during the day and moderate at night. Small mammals are more common. Songbirds are easily viewed, especially during the spring. Waterfowl are best viewed in late fall through early spring.

Directions: *Go five miles west on Interstate 20 from Colorado City, then south six miles on FM 2836 to park entrance.*

Ownership: TPWD (915-728-3931)
Size: 500 acres
Closest Town: Colorado City

15 BIG SPRING STATE PARK

Description: A mixture of species from three ecological regions can be viewed in this region. A small prairie dog town attracts hawks and burrowing owls (which also use the mounds) during early mornings and late afternoons. A nature trail offers bird and lizard watching and is a good introduction to native plants. Great horned owls, scaled quail, roadrunners, and scrub jays are present all year. Painted buntings and blue grosbeaks nest here in the summer. Mountain bluebirds, solitaires, three species of towhees, at least eight species of sparrows, and juncos winter in the park. Birds and small mammals can be viewed while driving or walking the Scenic Mountain Trail. Comanche Trail Park, just south of the state park, is the site of the "big spring" and offers good wildlife viewing.

Viewing Information: Viewing probability is high for prairie dogs, burrowing owls, lizards, and most songbirds.

Directions: *In Big Spring, 1.2 miles west of U.S. 87 and FM 700 intersection.*

Ownership: TPWD (806-263-4931)
Size: 370 acres
Closest Town: Big Spring

REGION 3: CROSS TIMBERS AND PRAIRIES

Early Texans named this region after the belts of blackjack and post oak forests that crossed strips of prairie. Most of the plants and animals seen here have ranges that extend northward into the great plains, or eastward into the forests. Native grasses have given way in many areas to species more tolerant of modern livestock grazing. The rolling landscape ranges from 500 to 1,500 feet; annual rainfall is from twenty-eight to thirty-five inches.

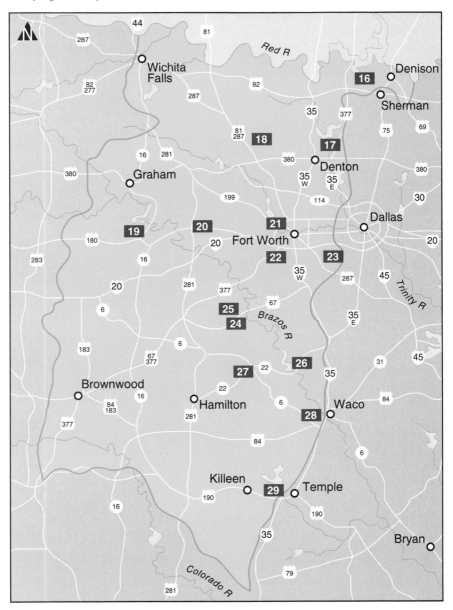

16	Hagerman National Wildlife Refuge	**23**	Dallas Nature Center
17	Lake Ray Roberts	**24**	Fossil Rim Wildlife Center
18	Lyndon B. Johnson National Grassland	**25**	Dinosaur Valley State Park
19	Possum Kingdom State Park	**26**	Lake Whitney State Park
20	Lake Mineral Wells State Park	**27**	Meridian State Park
21	Fort Worth Nature Center and Refuge	**28**	Waco Area
22	Benbrook Lake	**29**	Belton Lake

Description: The marsh, grassland, and open water habitats of this refuge attract thousands of waterfowl during fall, winter, and spring. Canada, white-fronted, snow, and Ross' geese winter here. Also look for mallards, pintails, green-winged teals, shovelers, blue-winged teals, redheads, canvasbacks, scaup, and ringnecks. Wading birds are prominent in the summer and many shorebirds migrate through in July. Woodland birds can be viewed in the bottomland hardwoods where white-tailed deer and small mammals also abound. Beaver are found in ponds behind the dam.

Viewing Information: Viewing probability is high for most aquatic species and small mammals. A self-guided auto tour and observation tower offer exceptional viewing opportunities. Songbird viewing is best during spring migration. Harris Creek Trail provides viewing of wildlife in bottomland and prairie habitats. Deer are occasionally seen. Beaver cuttings and lodges are easily seen but the animal is not.

Directions: *North from U.S. 82 near Sherman for four miles on FM 1417 to refuge road just north of Grayson County Airport. Follow signs on refuge road west for six miles to headquarters, where the auto tour and nature trail begin. Or drive north of U.S. 82 from Sadler on FM 901 for three miles, turn east and follow signs for eight miles to the refuge.*

Ownership: USFWS (903-786-2826)
Size: 11,320 acres
Closest Town: Sadler

The changing autumn colors at Hagerman National Wildlife Refuge offer a beautiful backdrop for viewing thousands of ducks and geese as they return from their northern breeding range. JOE COLE

17 LAKE RAY ROBERTS

Description: Three distinct habitats are featured at this site. On or near the lake, look for three species of geese, ducks, wading birds, marine birds, and shorebirds. Waterfowl are abundant and are best viewed from a boat. Grasslands host nine species of sparrows, other songbirds, small mammals, and wildflowers. Oak forests and savannahs provide habitat for migrating warblers, other songbirds, white-tailed deer, and small mammals.

Viewing Information: Late fall to early spring is best for waterfowl and sparrows. Shorebird viewing probability is moderate to high during migration in mid-summer. Viewing probability for most mammals is moderate. Culp Branch Native Prairie is just west of the dam but does not have trails. Isle duBois State Park is being developed just east of the dam. A trail is planned that will circle the lake, linking wildlife management units and state parks.

Directions: *Dam is six miles west of Sanger or three miles east of U.S. 377 on FM 455. Lake can be accessed from other county and state roads north of Sanger and Pilot Point.*

Ownership: ACOE (TPWD, 817-325-0359)
Size: 43,000 acres
Closest Town: Sanger

Although widespread in Texas, raccoons are strictly nocturnal and thus seldom seen. Their tracks, however, are often found near water, evidence of the previous night's hunt for crayfish. DENNIS HENRY

Description: Small lakes are found within the mosaic of grasslands and oaks that characterize the scattered management units of this national grassland. White-tailed deer, small mammals, coyotes, bobcats, red fox, waterfowl, bob-white quail, turkey, and songbirds thrive in the diverse habitats provided by this area.

Viewing Information: Waterfowl viewing is best during the winter, while the greatest diversity of songbirds are seen during the spring and fall migrations. The chances of observing carnivores are not high but can be improved by driving the roads at night or just after dawn. Hiking trails are being developed at Black Creek Recreation Site to enhance wildlife viewing opportunities. Do not trespass onto the private lands that surround most of the management units.

Directions: *Over forty management units are scattered in Wise County between FM 730 and U.S. 287 north of Decatur. Turn west from FM 730 and east from U.S. 287 on the county roads and drive until you see signs marking the national grass-land unit boundaries. A detailed map, available at Forest Service headquarters in Decatur, is needed to find specific units. To reach the Black Creek Recreation Site, drive about three miles north of Decatur on FM 730, turn north on Red Deer Road for about 3.5 miles, then west on Claborn Road for .6 mile. Turn north for about .5 mile then west for another quarter mile to reach the lake.*

Ownership: USFS (817-627-5475)
Size: 20,324 acres **Closest Town:** Alvord

The fiery color of tall grasses is a reminder of the importance of periodic fires to the ecology of this unique habitat. FRANK MOSTER

19 POSSUM KINGDOM STATE PARK

Description: A large colony of cliff swallows at Hell's Gate on scenic Possum Kingdom Lake provides a dramatic visual and acoustic display from March through June. Canyons and forests of shinnery oak and Ashe juniper provide preferred habitats for the endangered black-capped vireo and golden-cheeked warbler. White-tailed deer are abundant and easily photographed. Small mammals are common.

Viewing Information: Viewing probability is high for cliff swallows from March through June, high for deer and small mammals all year, and low for the endangered species.

Directions: Take U.S. 180 west from Fort Worth then seventeen miles north on PR 33. Hell's Gates is about twelve lake miles toward the dam from the park and can be reached only by boat.

Ownership: TPWD (817-549-1803)
Size: 1,529 acres
Closest Town: Caddo

20 LAKE MINERAL WELLS STATE PARK

Description: Wildlife highlights of this site are gray fox, ringtail, white-tailed deer, waterfowl, wild turkeys, and many species of songbirds. The park is known for its twenty-one miles of trails and geological formations.

Viewing Information: Gray fox and ringtail are most often seen on the less traveled roads at night but viewing probability is low. It is moderate for deer and turkey and high for waterfowl and songbirds during migration.

Directions: Three miles east of Mineral Wells or fourteen miles west of Weatherford on U.S. 180.

Ownership: TPWD (817-328-1171)
Size: 3,000 acres
Closest Town: Mineral Wells

Description: One of the largest urban nature centers in the country, this site is known for its wildlife and habitat diversity. Over twenty-five miles of hiking trails offer access to woodland, prairie, marsh, lake, and river bottom habitats. Reintroduced bison, white-tailed deer, coyotes, gray fox, skunks, beaver, raccoons, rabbits, pelicans, many kinds of wading birds and ducks, red-shouldered and red-tailed hawks, four species of owls, and such songbirds as prothonotary warblers and painted buntings can be viewed.

Viewing Information: Bison and deer are easily viewed in a large enclosure. Other land mammals are occasionally seen from the visitor center and trails. A long boardwalk over the lake provides excellent viewing of wading birds and waterfowl from late fall to early spring. Canoeing on the lake and river is one of the best ways to see aquatic wildlife. Beaver signs are common but the animal is seldom seen. Songbirds and hawks, but not owls, are frequently seen along the trails. Shorebirds and warblers are most diverse and easily viewed during spring and fall migrations.

Directions: *Drive two miles northwest of the Lake Worth bridge on Texas 199 to the intersection with FM 1886. Turn north into refuge entrance and proceed straight to visitor center.*

Ownership: City of Fort Worth (817-237-1111)
Size: 3,500 acres
Closest Town: Fort Worth

The Fort Worth Nature Center is an oasis for people and wildlife in the ever-expanding urban environment.

JOE COLE

22 BENBROOK LAKE

Description: This lake and surrounding habitats provide some of the best birding around Fort Worth. Birds of prey, waterfowl, wading birds, shorebirds, and songbirds plus beaver, nutria, and small mammals are featured. Paved roads and parks around the lake provide easy access to prairies, mud flats, shallow backwater areas, bottomland hardwoods, and the lake.

Viewing Information: Red-shouldered hawks, songbirds, and small mammals can be viewed along a trail in Holiday Park that leads to an observation blind where waterfowl, wading birds, shorebirds, and the occasional opsrey have been viewed. A shallow bay by the boat ramp in this park is particularly productive for aquatic birds. Rocky Creek and Mustang Parks also are good areas, especially for woodland species.

Directions: *Five miles southwest of Interstate 30 on U.S. 377 to Lakeside Drive. The dam is just east and Holiday Park is 4.3 miles south of this intersection. Rocky Creek and Mustang Parks are on the south shore.*

Ownership: ACOE (817-292-2400)
Size: 8,300 acres
Closest Town: Fort Worth

Watch for the beautiful osprey "hovering" above a lake or stream, then suddenly diving into the water to snare a fish. Reliant on fish, osprey are usually connected to water as they migrate through Texas. A few birds nest along the coast.

WENDY SHATTIL/BOB ROZINSKI

23 DALLAS NATURE CENTER

Description: A scenic and diverse urban park that offers a chance to see or hear black-capped vireos. Red-tailed hawk and other raptors, Harris' sparrows and many other songbirds, small mammals, an occasional coyote, and reptiles can be viewed here. Situated on the White Rock Escarpment, 4.5 miles of trails pass through rolling prairies, ponds, and oak-juniper woodlands.

Viewing Information: Moderate probability of seeing the vireo in the spring and early summer, when songbird viewing is best. Viewing is likely for raptors and small mammals all year and for Harris' sparrows in winter and spring. Wildflowers are celebrated with a festival in April.

Directions: From the intersection of U.S. 67 and Interstate 20 in Dallas, drive southwest on U.S. 67 for .6 mile. Go west on Wheatland Road for four miles to entrance.

Ownership: Greenhills Environmental Center, City of Dallas (214-296-1955)
Size: 400 acres
Closest Town: Dallas

24 FOSSIL RIM WILDLIFE CENTER

Description: Although endangered exotic wildlife from around the world attracts most visitors to this park, native mammals, birds, and reptiles can also be viewed. Raccoons, skunks, white-tailed deer, jackrabbits, armadillos, painted and indigo buntings, blue grosbeaks, Harris' and other winter sparrows, and migrant songbirds such as the endangered golden-cheeked warbler and black-capped vireo are present. Diverse viewing opportunities are provided by a nine-mile auto tour, a nature trail, an equestrian program, overnight safari camps, and "behind-the-scene" tours featuring such endangered native carnivores as red and gray wolves, and margay, a spotted cat of the tropics. Hummingbirds and songbirds are common at birdfeeders near the restaurant. Native flowers are abundant in the spring and early fall.

Viewing Information: Probability of viewing is moderate for most native species and high for the exotic species. The endangered birds are uncommon but can be heard singing in the spring and early summer from the oak-juniper forests along the trails.

Directions: Take U.S. 67 west from Interstate 35W to Glen Rose, then three miles west on U.S. 67 to FM 2008. Entrance is about three miles south on FM 2008.

Ownership: PVT (817-897-2960)
Size: 3,000 acres
Closest Town: Glen Rose

25 | DINOSAUR VALLEY STATE PARK

Description: Although native wildlife species abound here today, dinosaurs shook the earth here about 100 million years ago. Tracks are found in fifteen localities from three kinds of these ancient animals, including species with feet over three feet in length. Tracks reveal predation and herding behavior in dinosaurs. Coyotes, bobcats, skunks, raccoons, white-tailed deer, and small mammals currently leave their tracks throughout the park. Several western species of birds, like common poorwills, black-chinned hummingbirds, canyon and Bewick's wrens, and rufous-crowned sparrows, reach the eastern edge of their range near the park. Two endangered birds, the black-capped vireo and golden-cheeked warbler, are near the northernmost parts of their breeding range.

Viewing Information: High probability of viewing dinosaurs—at least their fossilized tracks. Low probability for coyotes and bobcats, moderate for other featured mammals. The two endangered birds are heard more often than seen in the spring and early summer. Moderate to high viewing probability for most spring migrant birds and winter sparrows.

Directions: *Take U.S. 67 west from Interstate 35W to Glen Rose, then FM 205 four miles north to PR 59 and entrance.*

Ownership: TPWD (817-897-4588)
Size: 1,523 acres
Closest Town: Glen Rose

Tracks often reveal the secrets of wildlife species difficult or impossible to view. Standing near these tracks at Dinosaur Valley State Park, you can almost hear the thunderous sounds of extinct dinosaurs while listening to the songs of two species of birds threatened with extinction today. LAURENCE PARENT

Description: An excellent example of cross timbers and grasslands. The lake attracts bald eagles and an abundance of waterfowl during winter. White-tailed deer, small mammals, wild turkeys, and wading birds are viewed all year. Shorebirds are present and songbirds are most diverse during spring and fall migrations. Wildflowers are abundant from spring through early fall.

Viewing Information: Waterfowl and eagles are best viewed from boats on the lake. Mammals and turkeys are commonly seen near trees from the road. Warbler viewing is good along primitive trails. Sparrows are most diverse and easily viewed in winter. Trees beneath the dam also offer good bird watching.

Directions: Take the Hillsboro exit from Interstate 35 just south of the split in Interstate 35, then follow Texas 22 west from Hillsboro for twelve miles to Whitney. The park is three miles west of Whitney on FM 1244.

Ownership: ACOE (TPWD, 817-694-3793)
Size: 955 acres
Closest Town: Whitney

The Rio Grande subspecies of the wild turkey is the most abundant of the three varieties found in Texas. All but eliminated by 1930, hunting regulations and reintroduction programs enabled these magnificent birds to come back. Over half a million Rio Grand wild turkeys now strut through Texas habitats.

SHERM SPOELSTRA

27 MERIDIAN STATE PARK

Description: Golden-cheeked warblers, an endangered species of the Hill Country, is near its northern breeding range at this park. At least eighteen additional species of warblers and three of vireos, plus fourteen sparrow species can be seen here. The endangered birds occur in the Ashe juniper/oak habitat, while many other birds are found in the bottom lands. Waterfowl, wading birds, and shorebirds abound in and around the lake where turtles can be seen basking on logs around the edge. Gray fox, raccoons, white-tailed deer, rabbits, and other small mammals live here. Six miles of hiking trails and five miles of peaceful roads pass through these habitats.

Viewing Information: Probability of hearing the endangered bird is moderate to high, if you know its songs. Viewing the bird is more difficult. Avoid disturbing nesting birds. Viewing is best for shorebirds and most warblers during migration. Waterfowl and sparrows are most abundant in winter. Mammal viewing is good except for foxes, which are not frequently seen.

Directions: Take the Hillsboro exit from Interstate 35 just south of the split in Interstate 35, then follow Texas 22 west to Meridian. Park is about three miles southwest of Meridian on Texas 22.

Ownership: TPWD (817-435-2536)
Size: 503 acres
Closest Town: Meridian

Ponds and small inlets of lakes—along with patience—combine for excellent wildlife viewing: turtles basking on logs, a great blue heron snagging a leopard frog, or perhaps a raccoon washing its paws as darkness approaches.
LAURENCE PARENT

Description: A surprising diversity of birds and bird watching opportunities exist in Cameron Park and other parks around Lake Waco. In winter, look for sharp-shinned and Cooper's hawks, brown creeper, blue-gray gnatcatcher, water pipit, hermit thrush, and seven species of sparrows. Waterfowl and marine birds are common on Lake Waco. Summer residents include chuck-will's-widow, black-chinned hummingbirds, barn and northern rough-winged swallows, red-eyed and white-eyed vireos, and dickcissels. Other birds are present all year, including three species of owls, many wading birds, and red-headed, red-bellied, and ladder-backed woodpeckers. Watch for white-tailed deer near the lake.

Viewing Information: Viewing probabilities are moderate to high for most featured groups during the appropriate seasons, low to moderate for raptors. Migrating shorebirds can be abundant around the lake and in flooded fields near Waco.

Directions: Take Fort Fisher/University Parks exit from Interstate 35 (just south of Brazos River) and drive 2.5 miles northwest on University Drive to Cameron Park. The north parks and shores of Lake Waco can be reached by driving west from Interstate 35 on Lake Shore Drive for about four miles to Airport Road, then north to FM 3051, west to the dead end, and north to the lake headquarters. Southern parks and shoreline can be reached by driving northwest about six miles from Interstate 35 on Texas 6 and looking for signs to the lake.

Ownership: Cameron Park (City of Waco, 817-750-5980), Lake Waco (ACOE, 817-756-5359)
Size: Cameron Park, 680 acres; Lake Waco, 7,270 surface acres
Closest Town: Waco

Dependent on lakes, rivers, and wetlands, the beautiful snowy egret can frequently be observed shuffling through shallow water in an effort to frighten prey out of hiding.
SHERM SPOELSTRA

29 BELTON LAKE

Description: The mixture of canyon wren songs, a liquid, descending series of "tews," with the chaotic twittering at a cliff swallow colony, entertains visitors along Cox's Hollow Trail at Miller Springs Nature Area, near the dam. The area also offers a mixture of geologic features, bottomland hardwoods, prairies, springs, and river habitats. White-tailed deer, gray and red foxes, coyotes, fox squirrels, armadillos, wild turkeys, owls, over a hundred other birds, and abundant wildflowers representing a mix of eastern and western species can be viewed here. Several other parks around the lake offer similar viewing opportunities. Finally, waterfowl, wading birds, bald eagles, and osprey can be viewed from several vantage points around the lake. The Miller Springs Nature Center is being developed.

Viewing Information: Most species are not easily viewed except for the deer, small mammals, and many birds. Waterfowl viewing is best during winter when eagles and osprey are present but uncommon. Cliff swallows are best viewed during the spring and summer before they migrate south.

Directions: *From Interstate 35 in Belton, take Texas 439 west for 2.5 miles to FM 2271, then go less than a mile northeast across dam to nature area.*

Ownership: ACOE (817-939-1829)
Size: Nature area, 260 acres; lake, 12,500 acres
Closest Town: Temple

A colony of cliff swallows with parents circling and dodging each other, feeding their young, and repairing their mud nests can provide a wildlife watching phenomenon. There are six additional species of swallows in Texas. W. PERRY CONWAY

REGION 4: BLACKLAND PRAIRIES

In this region, tall grasses such as big bluestem, little bluestem, Indiangrass, and agricultural plants grow well on deep, clay soils, made black and very fertile by stored organic matter. Almost all of the original 12,000,000 acres of blackland prairies have been converted to farm or ranchland. Many of the remaining pieces of prairie have been taken over by woody plants following the prevention of natural fires by man. The level-to-rolling terrain ranges from 250 to 700 feet in elevation; annual rainfall here varies from thirty to forty-five inches.

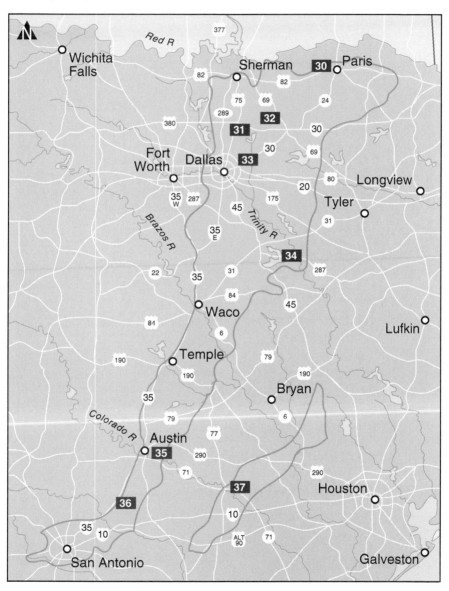

30	Gambill Goose Refuge	**34**	Richland Creek Wildlife Management Area
31	Heard Natural Science Museum and Wildlife Sanctuary	**35**	National Wildflower Research Center
32	Parkhill Prairie Preserve	**36**	A.E. Wood Fish Hatchery
33	Lake Ray Hubbard	**37**	Rice-Osborne Bird and Nature Trail

30 GAMBILL GOOSE REFUGE

Description: An average of about 3,000 (and as many as 7,000) wild Canada and snow geese, plus numerous species of ducks, winter on this attractive little refuge. Prairie birds, such as dickcissels and loggerhead shrikes, occur on the area surrounding the lake. Wildflowers are particularly impressive.

Viewing Information: Viewing wild geese is best from December through February. A captive flock can be seen anytime. Songbirds and wildflowers are most abundant in the spring and summer. Avoid roads after heavy rains.

Directions: Take FM 79 north from NW Loop 286 in Paris for 3.2 miles, then go west on FM 2820 for 1.5 miles. Turn north at refuge sign for .7 mile to lake.

Ownership: City of Paris (903-785-7511)
Size: 674 acres **Closest Town:** Paris

31 HEARD NATURAL SCIENCE MUSEUM AND WILDLIFE SANCTUARY

Description: Red-tailed and red-shouldered hawks, owls, and other raptors are seen along the trails and inside a raptor exhibit area. More than 270 species of birds occur in the ponds, creeks, prairies, and bottomland hardwoods, including twenty-nine warblers and twenty-one sparrows. Swamp rabbits, raccoons, squirrels, armadillos, reptiles, and wildflowers can also be easily viewed here.

Viewing Information: A five-mile network of trails offers diverse viewing opportunities. Small mammals and many birds can predictably be seen year-round. Warblers are best observed during the spring, while winter is the season for sparrows. Turtles and wading birds are easily viewed from the trail along Wilson Creek or from an observation area above a pond. Beaver signs are abundant near the creek but the animal is harder to see.

Directions: Take U.S. 75 north from Dallas to McKinney, then Texas 5 south to FM 1378. Turn east on FM 1378 for one mile to entrance.

Ownership: Heard Natural Science Museum and Wildlife Sanctuary (214-542-5566)
Size: 274 acres
Closest Town: McKinney

Description: Beautiful, unspoiled, and rare tallgrass prairie treats the wildlife viewer with a landscape similar to what must have been seen by early pioneers. Native wildflower diversity is reflected by color changes across the prairie and through the seasons. Insects also are diverse and active here. Red-tailed hawks, grasshopper and other sparrows, dickcissels, bobwhite quail, and mourning doves nest on or near the preserve. Coyotes, rabbits, skunks, armadillos, prairie kingsnakes and other snakes, lizards, and amphibians also are characteristic. An interesting upland species of crayfish can be easily viewed here.

Viewing Information: View songbirds, reptiles, amphibians, crayfish, and prairie flowers from spring through early fall. Hiking the nature trails through the rolling grasslands is enjoyable year-round. Probability of seeing mammals is moderate throughout the year, especially in early morning. Hawk viewing is always reliable during the day. Check with the Texas Nature Conservancy (512-224-8774) for permission to visit Clymer Meadow, a nearby prairie.

Directions: Take Texas 78 north from Dallas to U.S. 380, then east on 380 for about six miles. Turn north on FM 36 for nine miles, then west on County Road 1130 for one mile to entrance.

Ownership: Collin County (214-548-4653)
Size: 436 acres **Closest Town:** Merit

Walking through this tallgrass prairie liberates the senses and the imagination—an experience that changes markedly with the seasons, more subtly daily. The mood here can change quickly, as when lightning ignites a fire that, by burning the prairie, ensures its continued beauty. WILLIAM FRASER/COLLIN COUNTY OPEN SPACE

33 LAKE RAY HUBBARD

Description: Marshes around the lake meet the bottomlands of Rowlett Creek at the Woodland Basin Nature Area on the west side of the lake, offering diverse viewing opportunities. A boardwalk over the marsh provides close views of waterfowl, wading birds, shorebirds, songbirds, frogs, and fish. The forest trail and the nearby Rowlett Nature Trail are popular for watching such forest species as woodpeckers, chickadees, and other songbirds as well as squirrels and other small mammals. The large manmade lake attracts large numbers of waterfowl, gulls, and terns.

Viewing Information: Viewing probability for open-water birds is high on the lake during winter. Songbirds, easily viewed all year, are most abundant during spring and fall migrations. Probability of viewing is high all year for wading birds and small mammals.

Directions: *In Dallas, go north on Interstate 635 from Interstate 30 for about five miles, then east on Centerville Road 3.8 miles to Miller Road. Drive .5 mile east on Miller Road to entrance of Woodland Basin Nature Area.*

Ownership: City of Dallas (Garland Parks and Recreation, 214-205-2759)
Size: 22,745 acres
Closest Town: Dallas

What is that bullfrog saying at night with its deep, resonating call, audible a quarter of a mile away? It could be either "mo-re rain" or "kn-ee deep," depending on the weather. Or the bullfrog could be advertising its breeding territory to potential mates, as well as rivals. SHERM SPOELSTRA

34 RICHLAND CREEK WILDLIFE MANAGEMENT AREA

Description: This area combines the intense wildlife activity found around marshes with easy access to many viewing spots. The wetlands, swamps, and open water habitats attract large numbers of wading birds including wood storks, thousands of waterfowl, shorebirds, and songbirds. Bald eagles, osprey, and other raptors visit the area each winter. Beaver and mink are seen in marshes, and swamp rabbits and white-tailed deer are viewed along the roads.

Viewing Information: An extensive network of gravel roads provides easy access to marsh habitats and an observation tower is planned to aid the viewing of waterfowl. Viewing probability is high throughout the year for wading birds and small mammals and moderate for deer very early or late in the day. The probability is high for waterfowl and moderate for bald eagles and osprey during winter. Flocks of wood storks are most frequently viewed from mid- to late summer. Shorebirds and songbirds are most abundant during their spring and fall migrations. Although beaver signs are abundant, the chance of seeing the mammal during the day is slim, as it is for mink. Some roads become flooded after heavy rains. Wildlife viewing may be discouraged during the hunting season. Registration at headquarters and a Texas Conservation Passport are required for entry.

Directions: *From Corsicana, where U.S. 287 meets Interstate 45, drive southeast for twenty-five miles on U.S. 287 to entrance .5 mile east of dam and marked by signs. Viewing area is north of U.S. 287.*

Ownership: TPWD (903-928-2251)
Size: 13,700 acres **Closest Town:** Corsicana

P

Little blue herons are patient, methodical stalkers, feeding on minnows, frogs, and crayfish. Immatures have all-white plumage and are easily confused with young snowy egrets. Look for a paler, two-toned bill and dusky blue wing tips on the heron. JOHN SNYDER

35 | NATIONAL WILDFLOWER RESEARCH CENTER

Description: One of the best sites in the state for wildflowers, as well as butterflies, bees, other insects, and hummingbirds attracted to the plants. Three species of hummingbirds and thirty-five types of butterflies have been recorded at the site. Hawks and grassland birds, such as meadowlarks, dickcissels, and sparrows, also live here. Riparian woodlands nearby provide habitat for woodpeckers, blue jays, and other songbirds.

Viewing Information: Gardens are managed for native plants and research. Spring, summer, and fall produce different sets of flowers that attract distinct pollinators. Red-tailed hawks are observed at or near the site throughout the year. Sparrows are most abundant during winter. A visitor center, interpretive signs, and brochures offer educational opportunities.

Directions: *From U.S. 183 in Austin, take FM 969 east four miles, then FM 973 south for 1.5 miles to entrance.*

Ownership: National Wildflower Research Center (512-929-3600)
Size: Sixty acres
Closest Town: Austin

It seems easier to appreciate the important ecological connections of a grassland, perhaps because they take place at a visual level so accommodating to people. These connections, including those of pollinators and plants, are studied at the National Wildflower Research Center.

NATIONAL WILDFLOWER
RESEARCH CENTER

Description: An excellent place for close-up views of native and game fish during the various phases of their life-cycle. Look for largemouth bass, channel catfish, yellow catfish, striped bass, and rainbow trout, as well as paddlefish, which are endangered in Texas.

Viewing Information: Viewing probability is high for all species. Young paddlefish are viewed from March into August. Trout are present from December through February.

Directions: *One mile south of San Marcos on FM 621.*

Ownership: TPWD (512-353-0572)
Size: 118 acres
Closest Town: San Marcos

Paddlefish are strangely beautiful and intriguing, even as babies, which is how they may be seen at the A.E. Wood Fish Hatchery. See page fifteen for a drawing of an adult paddlefish, and ask hatchery personnel for details on the life history of this amazing fish that is unfortunately threatened with extinction.
GLENN MILLS/TEXAS PARKS AND WILDLIFE

37 RICE-OSBORNE BIRD AND NATURE TRAIL

Description: This cozy 2.5-mile trail meanders through or near four distinct habitats each with its own set of watchable wildlife, especially birds. Hermit thrush and Carolina chickadee are typical of woodlands in the winter. The prairie is preferred by scissor-tailed flycatcher and painted bunting in spring and summer and by the eastern bluebird all year. Tri-colored heron and red-winged blackbird are found in the marsh all year and American white pelicans, bufflehead, and other ducks spend winters on the lake. Osprey, crested caracara, and many other birds also occur at the site in the spring. White-tailed deer, squirrels, eastern cottontails, and raccoons also are reasonably common all year. Prairie wildflowers peak in the spring and early summer.

Viewing information: Viewing probability is low for osprey and caracara. Moderate to high for other featured species.

Directions: *From LaGrange, drive ten miles northeast on Texas 159 to Oak Thicket Park and nature trail entrance.*

Ownership: LCRA (409-968-5756, LaGrange Chamber of Commerce)
Size: Twenty acres
Closest Town: LaGrange

One of the state's most colorful songbirds, male painted buntings can be difficult to see because they hide in the vegetation of old fields, forest edges, and fence rows. One of the migratory species connecting Texas with Latin America, painted buntings may also be declining in numbers. JOHN SNYDER

REGION 5: POST OAK SAVANNAHS

This low rolling region is covered with a mixture of grassland and hardwood forests--oaks in the uplands, elms, hackberry, and cottonwood in the bottomlands. Almost all of the grasslands have been cultivated. Most of the animals also occur in either the prairies to the west or pine forests to the east. Elevations range from 200 to 500 feet; annual rainfall totals 30 to 45 inches.

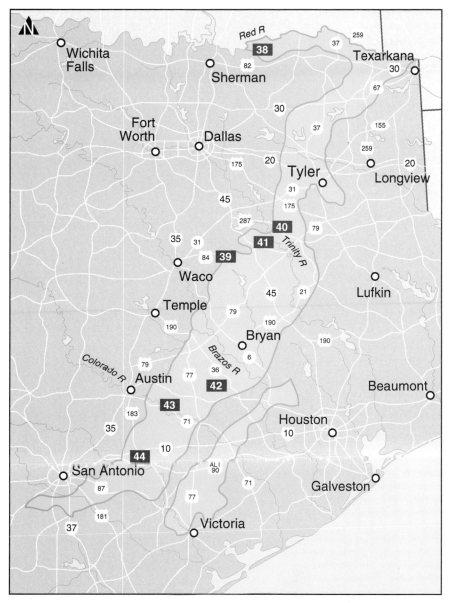

38	Caddo National Grassland	41	Fairfield Lake State Park
39	Fort Parker State Park	42	Lake Somerville State Park
40	Gus A. Engeling Wildlife	43	Bastrop State Park/Lake Bastrop
	Management Area	44	Palmetto State Park

38 CADDO NATIONAL GRASSLAND

Description: A mosaic of grasslands, oaks, pines, and cedar characterize the scattered management units that comprise this national grassland, which also includes several lakes. The area provides good habitat for white-tailed deer, small mammals, red and gray fox, waterfowl, ring-billed and Bonaparte's gulls, bobwhite quail, wild turkey, and other birds. More than 100 species of birds have been recorded during Christmas bird counts. Look for red and big brown bats foraging above open areas at dusk.

Viewing Information: Viewing probability is moderate to high for most of the wildlife of the region. Although songbird diversity peaks during spring migration, winter is the best time for sparrows and longspurs, as well as for eagles, geese, and other waterfowl. The chances of observing carnivores, including coyotes and bobcats, are not high but can be improved by driving the roads at night or just after dawn. Hiking trails are being developed to enhance wildlife viewing opportunities. Plan your visit so that it does not coincide with the deer hunting season. Please do not trespass onto the private lands that surround most of the management units.

Directions: *The core of the grassland is reached by driving west on U.S. 82 from Paris for twenty-one miles to Honey Grove, then north on Texas 100 for ten miles to Forest Road 919 (Bois d'Arc Springs Road). Turn west to enter the grassland and proceed to Lake Davy Crockett and Coffee Mill Recreation Sites. A detailed map, available at Forest Service headquarters in Bonham, is needed to find specific units.*

Ownership: USFS (817-627-5475)
Size: 17,796 acres
Closest Town: Selfs

Habitat diversity accounts for a great deal of the species diversity at the state and local levels. For instance, lakes, grasslands, and forests provide a patchwork of habitats that attract a surprising number of species to the Caddo National Grasslands. LAURENCE PARENT

Description: Eastern bluebirds and other songbirds are abundant in this park of gently rolling oak woodlands surrounding Lake Fort Parker. White-tailed deer, raccoons, squirrels, rabbits, and songbirds are common in the woodlands. Waterfowl and marine and wading birds use the lake.

Viewing Information: Mammals, wading birds, and some songbirds are easily viewed all year. Although most ducks and geese are winter migrants, wood ducks nest around the lake. Wood storks appear during late summer. Lake Mexia also should be checked for waterfowl. Old Fort Parker State Historic Site and the Confederate Reunion Grounds Park offer insights into the interesting history of this region.

Directions: *Take U.S. 84 west from Interstate 45 to Mexia, then Texas 14 south six miles to park.*

Ownership: TPWD (817-562-5751)
Size: 1,485 acres
Closest Town: Mexia

Wildlife watchers acquainted with the behavior of blue jays and crows may not be surprised to learn that these birds are related. The colorful and flamboyant blue jay produces a wide variety of calls, including some that mimic hawks.
JOHN SNYDER

40 | GUS A. ENGELING WILDLIFE MANAGEMENT AREA

Description: Rich with viewing opportunities, this site is also one of the most scenic representations of deciduous forest in east Texas. Habitats associated with Catfish Creek (a National Natural Landmark), spring-fed streams, sloughs, ponds, and bogs accentuate the hilly forest of oak, hickory, sweetgum, and elm. Understory plants include flowering dogwood, American beautyberry, and huckleberry. Several beaver ponds, a magnet for wildlife, enrich the region; one has a boardwalk, providing exceptional viewing of beaver, mink, ducks, song and wading birds, alligators, turtles, and fish. White-tailed deer, bobcats, both species of fox, skunks, and rabbits can be viewed here. The beautiful corn snake and eastern coachwhip are found here along with over thirty other species of snakes, numerous salamanders, and frogs.

Viewing Information: Most wildlife can be seen with moderate probability early in the morning or late in the evening from roads or trails. Mink, fox, and bobcats are seldom seen, while alligators are frequently viewed except during the colder months. Coachwhips and Texas rat snakes are common along roads during summer days. Ducks are abundant around water during the winter. Viewing is productive at the numerous dead trees, which provide cavities for wood ducks, woodpeckers, and the stunning prothonotary warbler. Most of the roads are unimproved and some require four-wheel drive when wet. Wildlife viewing may be discouraged during the hunting season. Registration at headquarters and a Texas Conservation Passport are required for entry.

Directions: *From Palestine where U.S. 287 and U.S. 79 intersect, go northwest twenty miles on U.S 287 to entrance.*

Ownership: TPWD (903-928-2251)
Size: 10,941 acres **Closest Town:** Palestine

Beavers are referred to as "keystone species" because they perform such an important role in the ecology of a region. Beavers create ponds, which provide diverse habitats for many species of wildlife. When beavers move, their abandoned ponds and adjacent clearings slowly regenerate, providing additional habitat types.

GRANT KLOTZ/N.E. STOCK PHOTO

41 FAIRFIELD LAKE STATE PARK

Description: Abundant bald eagles and white-tailed deer are the primary wildlife attractions of this park. Other wildlife include songbirds, waterfowl, and small mammals. Habitats vary from oak-hickory forests, with dogwood in the understory, to open prairies and a warm lake.

Viewing Information: Bald eagle viewing probability is high during the winter with an average of twenty-two eagles. Eagles are best observed from boats but can also be seen with binoculars and spotting scopes from several places along the shore. Deer and small mammals are easily seen from the roads or along the more than six miles of hiking trails. Songbird watching is best during the spring, waterfowl during the winter.

Directions: From Interstate 45 take Texas 84 east to Fairfield, then go six miles northeast via FM 488 and FM 2570 to PR 64.

Ownership: TPWD (903-359-3926)
Size: 1,400 acres
Closest Town: Fairfield

42 LAKE SOMERVILLE STATE PARK

Description: Bird and mammal diversities here are associated with habitats that vary from bottomland hardwoods, thickets, prairies, mud flats, and open water of the lake. White-tailed deer, coyotes, small mammals, red-shouldered hawks, three species of owls, and many songbirds are resident here. Waterfowl, bald eagles, and osprey winter here and shorebirds migrate through the area.

Viewing Information: The two units of the park, Birch Creek on the north shore and Nails Creek on the south, are connected by a twenty-one-mile hiking/equestrian trail system. Wildlife viewing probabilities are good along this trail, on eight miles of nature trails, and on the lake. Owls, of course, are heard more often than seen.

Directions: The Birch Creek Unit is reached by taking FM 60 south for seven miles from Lyons on Texas 36, then PR 57 five miles south to park. Take U.S. 290 seven miles east from U.S. 77, then FM 180 north for fifteen miles to Nails Creek Unit.

Ownership: ACOE (TPWD, 409-289-7763 and 409-289-2392)
Size: 940 acres
Closest Town: Somerville

43 BASTROP STATE PARK AND LAKE BASTROP

Description: The "Lost Pines of Texas," a stand of loblolly pine isolated from the pineywoods region by about 180 miles, is featured at this picturesque area. Typical pineywoods species, such as pileated woodpecker, several warblers, and the melodious wood thrush, nest here. The toylike calls of red-breasted nuthatches can usually be heard in the winter. The sandy soils of the area also are preferred by Houston toads, an endangered species. White-tailed deer, squirrels, raccoons, and rabbits are common. Ducks, geese, and a few osprey winter at nearby Lake Bastrop, which is being developed as a state park. Departure and arrival activities at a roosting colony of double-crested cormorants provide an interesting wildlife display at this lake.

Viewing Information: The viewing probability for most birds and mammals is high while driving park roads or hiking the 8.5 miles of trails. Toads are most easily heard and seen between February and June. Scenic PR 1 connects Bastrop with Buescher State Park and crosses Allum Creek, one of the best birding sites.

Directions: *Take U.S. 71 east from Austin for about thirty miles to just east of Bastrop, then Texas 21 north for about a mile to the park entrance. Entrances to the south and north shores of Lake Bastrop are two and four miles north of park entrance on Texas 21.*

Ownership: TPWD, Park (512-321-2101); LCRA, Lake Bastrop (512-321-3307)

Size: 3,500 acres
Closest Town: Bastrop

Of the ten toad species in Texas, the most endangered and controversial is the Houston toad, confined to a small area betwen Austin and Houston. This toad requires sandy soil for burrowing and pools of water for breeding—a type of habitat threatened by a variety of land use practices. JAMES GODWIN

Description: Sulphur-laden water, artesian wells, oxbow lakes, cordgrass marshes, bottomland hardwoods, swamps, and open meadows give a tropical feel to this unique park. Renowned for its botanical and wildlife diversity, over 500 species of plants and 240 kinds of birds are recorded here. Wood duck, red-shouldered hawk, great horned and barred owls, prothonotary warbler, and painted bunting nest in the park, which also is used extensively by spring migrants. Winter brings brown creeper, pine siskin, and more than ten species of sparrows. White-tailed deer, armadillos, raccoons, turtles, and squirrels are abundant.

Viewing Information: Viewing is reliable for most resident species and many of the migratory species along the roads or 1.5 miles of nature trails. Ducks are most likely near the oxbow lakes or San Marcos River.

Directions: *Take U.S. 183 south from Interstate 10 near Luling for 2.4 miles to entrance.*

Ownership: TPWD (512-672-3266)
Size: 264 acres **Closest Town:** Luling

Red-eared sliders, one of the thirty-five species of turtles in Texas, are also one of the most widespread, occurring over most of the state east of the Pecos River. They are also one of the most easily observed, basking on logs in quiet waters. The distinctive red mark behind each ear may become obscured with age. GEORGE H. H. HUEY

With beautiful flowers, diverse wildlife, and lush vegetation, Palmetto State Park (previous page) looks and feels tropical. The dwarf palmettos are one of only two native species of palms in Texas. LAURENCE PARENT

REGION 6: PINEYWOODS

Rolling hills with forests of pines and oaks, and bottomlands rich with tall hardwoods distinguish this region. Species composition varies with the extent of flooding. Commercial forestry and agricultural practices have altered much of the pine woodlands, while construction of lakes and land clearing have removed all but remnants of the bottomlands. Old pine stands that remain are home to the red-cockaded woodpecker. The white blossoms of flowering dogwoods announce the coming of spring. Elevations range from 200 to 700 feet; annual rainfall varies from forty to fifty-six inches.

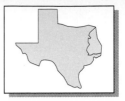

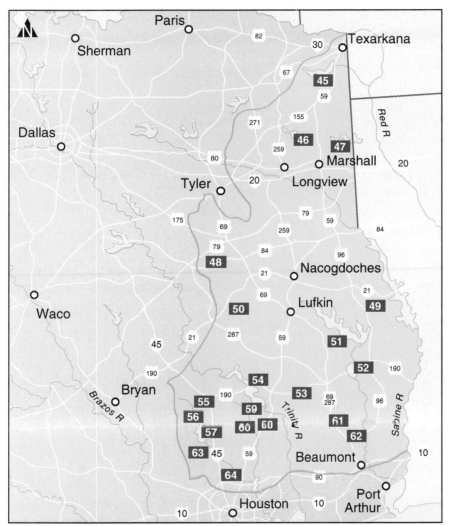

45	Atlanta State Park
46	Lake of the Pines
47	Caddo Lake State Park
48	Fairchild State Forest/Texas State Railroad
49	Pine Park Rest Area
50	Four C National Recreation Trail
51	Boykin Springs Recreation Area
52	Martin Dies, Jr. State Park
53	Alabama/Coushatta Indian Reservation
54	Lake Livingston/U.S. 190 Causeway

55	Hunstville State Park
56	Cagle Recreation Area
57	Red-cockaded Woodpecker Interpretive Site
58	Big Creek Scenic Area
59	Double Lake Recreation Area
60	San Jacinto River Canoe Trail
61	Big Thicket National Preserve
62	Roy E. Larson Sandyland Sanctuary
63	Jones State Forest
64	Jesse Jones Nature Center

45 ATLANTA STATE PARK

Description: This park features swamp and cottontail rabbits, gray and fox squirrels, armadillos, raccoons, and white-tailed deer. Forest songbirds, such as brown creepers and brown thrashers, wood thrush, many warblers and vireos, cardinals, and woodpeckers also are common. Along the hiking and nature trails, listen for the loud flutelike song of wood thrush in summer and the nasal, toy hornlike call of the red-breasted nuthatch during winter. Frogs, toads, and salamanders can be found on the forest floor or breeding in temporary ponds during early spring.

Viewing Information: Viewing probability throughout the year is high for small mammals and moderate at night for larger species. Songbird viewing also is good all year but best between spring and fall migrations.

Directions: Drive north from Atlanta on U.S. 59 to just north of Queen City, turn west on FM 96 for eight miles to FM 1154, then north for two miles to the park entrance.

Ownership: TPWD (903-796-6476)
Size: 1,475 acres
Closest Town: Atlanta

The swamp rabbit and eastern cottontail both occur in east Texas. The larger swamp rabbit (left) is distinguished from the cottontail by its pinkish-cinnamon eyering and brownish body color; cottontails have whitish eyering and a grayish coat. Swamp rabbits are usually the more numerous species in the bottomlands and marshes, but seldom occur in the uplands, where cottontails flourish. PHOTOS BY GRADY ALLEN

Description: This scenic lake is one of the best places to see bald eagles, with more than thirty individuals present during the winter. Common loons, horned grebes, Bonaparte's gull, and diving ducks such as canvasbacks, common goldeneye, bufflehead, and lesser scaup are typical winter visitors. The pine forests surrounding the lake harbor many songbirds best viewed with binoculars.

Viewing Information: Bald eagle viewing probability is high in the winter, especially at the Dam Overlook. Waterfowl viewing from a boat or on the shore is excellent during the winter. Songbirds, most diverse during migration, are easily viewed all year.

Directions: *Take Texas 49 northwest from Jefferson on U.S. 59 for about three miles, then west on FM 729 to where it intersects with FM 726. Go south on FM 726 to reach the dam and parks on the southern shore, or continue west on FM 729 to parks on the north shore.*

Ownership: ACOE (903-665-3229)
Size: 18,700 surface acres
Closest Town: Jefferson

47 **CADDO LAKE STATE PARK**

Description: Swamp scenes and associated wildlife characterize this park located on what was once the South's largest natural lake (now dammed). American alligator, beaver, swamp rabbit, wood duck, red-shouldered hawk, fish crow, Louisiana waterthrush, Swainson's warbler, yellow-throated warbler, and cypress trees covered with Spanish moss are typical. Boats driven through the maze of channels and bayous are the only means of travel to thousands of acres of cypress groves. Hiking trails and an excellent nature trail offer owls, white-tailed deer, and abundant small mammals.

Viewing Information: Alligator, beaver, and owls are seldom seen; wood ducks, deer, small mammals, and fish crows easily observed. Yellow-throated warblers and other songbirds are easily observed from spring to early fall. Swainson's warbler and the waterthrush are more difficult to view.

Directions: *Drive fourteen miles northeast of Marshall on Texas 43, then one mile east on FM 2198 to entrance.*

Ownership: TPWD (210-679-3351)
Size: 3,480 acres
Closest Town: Karnack

The wood duck is the most abundant breeding duck in the eastern United States. It is found in bottomland hardwoods and other woodlands adjacent to water.
DAVID J. SAMS

48 FAIRCHILD STATE FOREST AND TEXAS STATE RAILROAD

Description: This state forest is probably the site nearest to Dallas where red-cockaded woodpeckers and Bachman's sparrows can be viewed. The largest of the numerous management units contains a large stand of shortleaf pines. White-tailed deer, squirrels, rabbits, and many birds occupy this forest. Many of these animals can occasionally be glimpsed from the turn-of-the-century steam-powered train as it passes through several of the forest units during its fifty-mile round trip between Rusk and Palestine state parks. Wildflower viewing from the train is particularly pleasing in the spring. Rusk State Park has a small lake where beaver signs, wood ducks, and water snakes are seen.

Viewing Information: Viewing probability is moderate to high for the woodpeckers, low for the sparrows. Small mammals and birds are easily viewed; deer are less common. Reservations should be made for the train ride. Additional facilities are available on the train and at the parks.

Directions: The large unit of state forest is about seventeen miles east of Palestine on U.S. 84. Train depots are in Rusk and Palestine State Parks, just west of Rusk and east of Palestine, respectively.

Ownership: Texas State Forest Service (903-586-7545); TPWD (903-683-2561)
Size: 2,750 acres in forest; 100 acres in parks
Closest Town: Rusk

49 PINE PARK REST AREA

Description: One of the easiest places to see red-cockaded and four other species of woodpeckers, as well as other species like American kestrel, Carolina chickadee, and tufted titmouse, that roost or nest in cavities. The loblolly pines in this picnic area are the oldest in the region and riddled with cavities important to wildlife. Eastern cottontails and armadillos also are here.

Viewing Information: This is an excellent bird watching site for people confined to a car because most birds can be viewed from the paved auto loop. Probability of viewing is high all year.

Directions: Take U.S. 96 north from Jasper for thirty-two miles to intersection with Texas 184, then six miles east on 184 to intersection with FM 2024 and park.

Ownership: State Department of Transportation (409-634-4433)
Size: Ten acres
Closest Town: Hemphill

50 FOUR C NATIONAL RECREATION TRAIL

Description: This scenic twenty-mile trail offers an opportunity to view representative wildlife of the region and experience typical pineywood habitats. Featured species include wood duck, red-shouldered hawk, barred owl, woodpeckers (pileated, endangered red-cockaded, and others), wood and hermit thrushes, three species of nuthatches, red-eyed and yellow-throated vireos, and numerous warblers. Also watch for bobcat, raccoon, white-tailed deer, gray and fox squirrels, armadillo, eastern cottontail and swamp rabbits, and red bats.

Viewing Information: The trail, which originates at Ratcliff Recreation Area and ends at the Neches Overlook, passes through part of the Big Slough Wilderness Area, which features a separate canoe trail. The recreation area has a lake and interpretive trails that should be visited. Viewing probability is low for the bobcat and red-cockaded woodpecker; moderate for brown-headed nuthatch, hawks, and owls; and high for other species. The wood thrush, vireos, and warblers are not present in winter. Red bats can be viewed flying twenty to thirty feet above ground in forest clearings.

Directions: *Take U.S. 69 north from Lufkin for twelve miles, then Texas 7 for twenty miles east to Ratcliff Recreation Area. To reach the north end of the trail from Ratcliff, take FM 227 eleven miles northwest to Texas 21, then go northeast on Texas 21 for six miles to Forest Service Road 511-3. Turn south on 511-3 for a mile, then east to the overlook.*

Ownership: USFS (409-544-2046)
Size: Twenty miles
Closest Town: Kennard

The presence of pileated woodpeckers is announced by their loud, jungle-like calls and the deep drumming sound they make when hammering on trees. This is the largest woodpecker in the United States, now that the ivory-billed woodpecker is thought to be extinct.

JOHN SNYDER

Description: One of the most scenic sites to see red-cockaded woodpeckers, pine warblers, Bachman's sparrow, and pitcher plants throughout the year. The open forest of loblolly pines is also home for four other woodpeckers, white-breasted and brown-headed nuthatches, blue jay, Carolina chickadee, and tufted titmouse. Winter flocks of the latter two species and nuthatches are occasionally joined by yellow-breasted sapsuckers as they search for insects in trees. At least ten species of warblers nest in the pines or hardwoods along Sawmill Trail and many others are seen during migration. Fox and gray squirrels, eastern cottontail, and armadillos also are common.

Viewing Information: Viewing probability for featured species is high. Some species of warblers may be difficult to find.

Directions: *South from Lufkin on U.S. 69 to Zavalla, then Texas 63 south for 11.5 miles to Forest Service Road 313. Turn right and drive 1.3 miles to Forest Service Road 313A, turn right again for .3 mile to trail on left leading through red-cockaded woodpecker site. Continue on Forest Service 313A for about a quarter of a mile to gate and follow signs to pitcher plant bogs. Continue on 313 to recreation area where Sawmill Trail begins.*

Ownership: USFS (409-639-8620)
Size: 300 acres
Closest Town: Jasper

A 1929 quote says that the gray squirrel "supplies the city man, the farm boy, and the sportsman the most alluring motive for a glorious tramp in the ever-inspiring woods." Of course, the quote could also apply to women of all ages and backgrounds.
MASLOWSKI PHOTO

52 MARTIN DIES, JR. STATE PARK

Description: One of the wildlife viewing treasures of the region, this beautiful park and surrounding area includes pine and bottomland hardwood forests, open waters of B.A. Steinhagen Lake, swamps, and rivers. A large colony of wading birds with up to 20,000 nests is in the middle of the lake just south of U.S. 190 and can be viewed with binoculars or a spotting scope from the south Cherokee unit of the park or from a boat in the lake. Several other colonies are located in the Angelina-Neches Scientific Unit and Dam B Wildlife Management Unit on the north side of the lake. Snowy and cattle egrets, little blue and tri-colored herons, white ibises, anhingas, and yellow-crowned night-herons are common. Abundant waterfowl in the winter; alligators and bull frogs in the summer. Most of the typical pineywood birds and mammals can be viewed from the nature trails all year. Fall colors are striking.

Viewing Information: Most featured species are easily seen from a boat on the lake or trails in the park. The colonies and management units can be reached only by boat. Please do not disturb nesting or roosting birds by approaching too closely.

Directions: *Entrance to headquarters in the south unit is seventeen miles east of junction with U.S. 69 on U.S. 190, or twelve miles west from Jasper on U.S. 190. Obtain map to locate trails and boat ramps.*

Ownership: ACOE (TPWD, 409-384-5231)
Size: 705 acres in park; 15,000-acre lake   **Closest Town:** Jasper

Thousands of wading birds frequently nest in colonies known as rookeries. Rookeries are usually over water and may involve ten or more species, including the great blue heron shown here. Viewers should remain quiet and far enough away so as not to disturb nesting or roosting birds.

MARK PICARD/N.E. STOCK PHOTO

53 ALABAMA AND COUSHATTA INDIAN RESERVATION

Description: An excellent site for people confined to cars for viewing the endangered-cockaded woodpecker; several colonies are located near the residential area and village center. Other woodpeckers, kingfishers, nuthatches, chickadees, crows, blue jays, warblers, raccoons, squirrels, rabbits, and white-tailed deer also can be viewed around the lake or along the nature trails. Wading birds and an occasional bald eagle are viewed on Lake Tombigbee.

Viewing Information: Viewing probability is high for woodpeckers and other featured species except eagles, which are uncommon. One woodpecker colony is found near the entrance and another occurs at the southwest corner of the lake spillway. Check with forestry headquarters for information on other colonies.

Directions: *Entrance is about sixteen miles east of Livingston and sixteen miles west of Woodville on U.S. 190.*

Ownership: Alabama and Coushatta Indian Reservation (409-563-4391)
Size: 4,600 acres
Closest Towns: Livingston and Woodville

54 LAKE LIVINGSTON/U.S. 190 CAUSEWAY

Description: A site for spectacular bird flights. As many as 25,000 purple martins roost beneath the two-mile U.S. 190 bridge over the lake where they mass together about half an hour after sunset from June through August. From November through April, about 10,000 double-crested cormorants fly to (in the evening) and from (in the morning) their roosting area. The bridge also is a good place to view gulls, terns, and waterfowl during the winter.

Viewing Information: Viewing probability is high for selected species during the recommended times and seasons. Parking is allowed on designated parts of the causeway but use extreme caution.

Directions: *Causeway is on U.S. 190 about twenty-six miles east of Interstate 45 at Huntsville, or about eleven miles west of U.S. 59 at Livingston.*

Ownership: State Department of Transportation (409-634-4433)
Size: Two miles
Closest Town: Onalaska

55 HUNTSVILLE STATE PARK

Description: The combination of good wildlife viewing, excellent nature trails designed for wildlife viewing, and useful exhibits about wildlife diversity makes this one of the premier sites in the state. White-tailed deer, raccoons, armadillos, and squirrels are typical mammals that can be viewed. Twelve species of warblers—including prothonotary, hooded, and Swainson's—nest here, as do three species of woodpeckers, three species of vireos, two species of buntings, white-breasted and brown nuthatches, flycatchers, red-shouldered hawks, and wood ducks. An occasional alligator can be observed in the lake.

Viewing Information: Featured mammals and most birds are easily seen. Some of the songbirds are not present in the winter and some, like Swainson's warbler and brown-headed nuthatches, are more difficult to view. Probability of seeing an alligator is low.

Directions: *Drive six miles south of Huntsville on Interstate 45 and take exit 109 to PR 40 and the entrance.*

Ownership: TPWD (409-295-6544)
Size: 2,083 acres
Closest Town: Huntsville

56 CAGLE RECREATION AREA

Description: A beaver pond and lodge offer a good opportunity to observe the handiwork of these interesting aquatic mammals. Small numbers of waterfowl and wading birds also use the pond.

Viewing Information: Although signs of beaver activity are abundant, the probability of actually viewing the beavers is low because they are active at night.

Directions: *Take the New Waverly exit off of Interstate 45 and travel about 5.5 miles west to recreation site on FM 1375. From recreation site, turn left and drive about .8 mile to beaver pond on left. Use caution when parking on the side of road.*

Ownership: USFS (409-344-6205)
Size: Five acres
Closest Town: New Waverly

RED-COCKADED WOODPECKER INTERPRETIVE SITE

Description: A superb locality for viewing red-cockaded woodpeckers and their habitats and nesting trees, which are marked with green bands. A sign and information box help the wildlife viewer learn more about these birds and why they are endangered. The open pine forest with grass and shrub understory also provides habitat for Bachman's sparrows. Other woodpeckers, nuthatches, chickadees, and warblers are present. Wildflowers are beautiful in the spring and fall.

Viewing Information: Red-cockaded woodpeckers are easily seen, especially early and late in the day. Viewing probability for Bachman's sparrow is low but listen for warbling song from late-March through mid-May.

Directions: Travel 4.7 miles west on FM 1375 from the New Waverly exit off of Interstate 45. Parking area and woodpecker sign are on the south side of road.

Ownership: USFS (409-344-6205)
Size: About 100 acres   **Closest Town:** New Waverly

The red-cockaded woodpecker is an endangered species largely restricted to open forests with old pine trees that have heart disease, a condition that allows the birds to bore holes inside living trees. Den trees are recognized by the white sheet of pitch seeping from small holes bored around the den entrance.
JOHN SNYDER

58 BIG CREEK SCENIC AREA

Description: Beautiful bottomland hardwoods surrounded by pines and embracing a shallow, clear stream provide habitats for swamp rabbits, gray and fox squirrels, white-tailed deer, armadillos, and raccoons. The sights and sounds of red-shouldered hawk, pileated woodpecker, white-breasted nuthatch, American crow, blue jay, Swainson's and prothonotary warblers, and wood thrush treat the wildlife viewer during summer. Migrating warblers and butterflies flash through sun spots along the trails. Toads, frogs, and salamanders crawl beneath material on the forest floor or jump into the creek. Several loop trails offer diverse viewing opportunities. A five-mile trail connects the scenic area with Double Lake Recreation Area.

Viewing Information: Viewing probabilities are moderate to high for most mammals; low to moderate for deer, red-shouldered hawks, and prothonotary warblers; low for Swainson's warblers and salamanders; high for other birds, butterflies, and leopard frogs.

Directions: *From Cleveland on U.S. 59, go north on FM 2025 for ten miles, then turn east on FM 2666 for 2.5 miles, and go north on Forest Service 221, a gravel road. After .5 mile, turn east on Forest Service 217 for one mile to parking area.*

Ownership: USFS (713-592-6461)
Size: 1,450 acres   **Closest Town:** Cleveland

As the name "pine warbler" implies, this is a bird of the pineywoods. This is a unique warbler in that it both breeds and winters in east Texas. Most other warblers breed in the United States or Canada and then migrate across or around the Gulf of Mexico to spend the winter in Latin America. JOHN SNYDER

59 DOUBLE LAKE RECREATION AREA

Description: A trail around the twenty-three-acre lake provides viewing of a beaver pond below the dam and opportunities to see fox squirrel, swamp rabbit, armadillo, red-shouldered hawk, northern flicker, Carolina wren, and common yellowthroat. A boardwalk across the marshy upper end of the lake allows close views of fish, basking turtles, wading birds, aquatic invertebrates, and marsh plants. Typical pineywood species are viewed around campgrounds.

Viewing Information: Beaver, although active all year, are seldom seen. The best chances are very early in the morning. Red-shouldered hawks and common yellowthroats are not frequently viewed. Most other species are easily observed.

Directions: From Cleveland on U.S. 59, go north on FM 2025 for fifteen miles to entrance road. Turn east for one mile to lake and trail.

Ownership: USFS (713-592-6461)
Size: 544 acres   **Closest Town:** Cleveland

River otters were once found throughout much of east Texas and the upper coast. Because their habitats along rivers and streams have been altered, otters are uncommon today. Even in coastal areas, where they are most abundant, otters are shy and difficult to see. D. ROBERT FRANZ

60 | SAN JACINTO RIVER CANOE TRAIL

Description: A scenic and challenging canoe trip with wildlife viewing possibilities around each bend. Featured species include river otter, white-tailed deer, raccoons, gray squirrels, swamp rabbits, and numerous birds associated with bottomlands including green-backed heron, red-shouldered hawk, belted kingfisher, Swainson's warbler, plus the beautiful hooded and prothonotary warblers. Fall floats also offer beautiful autumn colors.

Viewing Information: Viewing probability is low for river otter and moderate to high for the other species. Songbird diversity is highest and warbler viewing is possible only from spring through early fall. The trail begins where the East Fork of the San Jacinto crosses Forest Service 293 and canoes can be taken out where the river crosses Forest Service 945. Some portage may be required to pass over downed trees. Spring and fall offer the best water conditions. Call Forest Service before making the trip to confirm water conditions because the river floods occasionally and may become too shallow during dry periods.

Directions: From Cleveland, drive north 10.5 miles on FM 2025, then turn west on Forest Service 293 (Upper Vann Road) for 1.8 miles to the East Fork of the San Jacinto River where trail begins. To reach the take out site, go north from Cleveland on FM 2025 for about five miles, then west on FM 945 for about .5 mile to the river.

Ownership: USFS (713-592-6461)
Size: Ten miles   **Closest Town:** Cleveland

One of our most pleasant summer sounds is that of a singing mockingbird, the state bird of Texas. The scientific name, *Mimus polyglottos*, means mimic of many tongues. Some individuals mimic, or mock, more than fifty different bird species as well as other sounds, like a dinner bell.

Description: In recognition of its international importance, the Big Thicket was designated a Biosphere Reserve in 1981. It has been referred to as "an American ark" and "a biological cross-roads" acknowledging the variety of habitats and species that coexist here. Old-growth pine forests, upland and bottomland hardwoods, meadows, bogs, and cypress sloughs maintain eighty-five species of trees, eleven of which are oaks, and nearly 1,000 flowering plants, including seventeen varieties of orchids and four types of insect-eating plants. Animals too are diverse but many are seldom viewed in the thick vegetation. There are forty-one species of mammals, nearly 300 of resident and migrant birds, sixty reptiles, and twenty-nine amphibians spread across the different habitats. Bobcats, coyotes, skunks, white-tailed deer, armadillos, squirrels, and rabbits are widespread, as are numerous species of bats. Red-shouldered hawks are common. Pileated, hairy, downy, red-bellied, red-headed, and red-cockaded woodpeckers occur here. Black and white, yellow-throated, and hooded warblers are found throughout the preserve; prothonotary and Swainson's warblers and American redstart live in the bottomlands. Louisiana waterthrush are found along upland sandy bottom streams, worm-eating warblers in acid bog baygall wetlands, prairie warblers and painted buntings in longleaf pine-savannahs, and Bachman's sparrows in mature pine forests.

Viewing Information: Probability of viewing is low for carnivores, bats, red-cockaded woodpecker, Louisiana waterthrush, redstart, and Swainson's and worm-eating warblers. It is moderate for hairy and red-headed woodpeckers, prairie warbler, Bachman's sparrow, and deer. Small mammals and most other featured birds are easily observed. The preserve, divided into eight land units and four river or stream corridors, features eight hiking trails. Kirby Nature Trail passes through a mixture of habitats and has a guide book. Sundew Trail, accessible to the physically challenged, crosses a pitcher plant bog and is a premier wildflower trail. Big Sandy Creek Horse Trail, designed for horses, hikers, and bicycles, winds through upland areas. The Neches River Canoe Trail, divided into segments of various lengths, offers waterfowl and wading bird viewing and a slim chance to see beavers and river otters.

Directions: *Detailed maps to the preserve units are available from headquarters in Beaumont and the visitor center. From the junction of U.S. 69 and U.S. 96 north of Beaumont, drive about twenty-two miles north on U.S. 69. Turn east on FM 420 for 2.9 miles to visitor center and Kirby Nature Trail.*

Ownership: NPS (409-839-2689)
Size: 86,000 acres
Closest Town: Beaumont

Habitat diversity means high species diversity, and the Big Thicket National Preserve has both. It also offers a variety of trails—for canoes, horses, hiking, and the physically challenged. LAURENCE PARENT

62 ROY E. LARSEN SANDYLAND SANCTUARY

Description: Tracks in the sand made by bobcats, coyotes, red fox, white-tailed deer, armadillos and other small mammals, roadrunners, northern bobwhite, songbirds, lizards, and snakes reveal the outstanding diversity of wildlife on this preserve. The coarse sand over much of the area drains water quickly, producing a savannah of longleaf pines, cactus, and other drought-resistant, fire-adapted plants. Additional habitats include bald cypress and water tupelo swamps, ponds, sphagnum bogs, and the poorly drained baygall community. These diverse habitats support one of the greatest varieties of wildflowers in the Big Thicket, including orchids, insect-eating plants, and flowering dogwood.

Viewing Information: Tracks are abundant but viewing probability for large mammals, except deer, is low. Birds are easier to see. During the summer, fence lizards, six-lined racerunners, and ground skinks are frequently observed, while eastern coachwhips, eastern hognose, copperheads, and other snakes are occasionally viewed. Six miles of hiking trails, an interpretive display, and a trail booklet enhance the wildlife viewing. An eight-mile canoe trail on Village Creek provides enjoyable viewing of bottomland wildlife, including a slim chance of observing a river otter or beaver. Please stay on trails to avoid damaging fragile sites.

Directions: *Drive north from Beaumont on U.S. 96 to Silsbee. Turn west for 2.5 miles on Texas 327 to entrance and trailhead. The canoe trail starts on the northern boundary of the preserve where Village Creek meets FM 418.*

Ownership: Texas Nature Conservancy (409-385-0445)
Size: 2,380 acres   **Closest Town:** Silsbee

Although many people needlessly fear all snakes, most species are harmless and some, like the Mexican milk snake and prairie ring-necked snake, are rather attractive. Many are important to the ecology of an area. Rattlesnakes, for instance, help control rodent populations.

63 JONES STATE FOREST

Description: This site features red-cockaded woodpecker, brown-headed nuthatch, Bachman's sparrow, white-tailed deer, and small mammals. The Sweetleaf Nature Trail winds through pine forests. Trail guide and key to gate are available at the headquarters.

Viewing Information: Viewing probability is high all year for featured species, except Bachman's sparrow, which is an uncommon winter visitor.

Directions: Drive about thirty-five miles north of Houston on Interstate 45 to FM 1488 and go west for 1.5 miles to headquarters and trailhead.

Ownership: Texas Forest Service (409-273-2261)
Size: 1,700 acres
Closest Town: Conroe

64 JESSE JONES NATURE CENTER

Description: Viewing and hearing the secretive Swainson's and beautiful prothonotary warblers are easier here than any other site because a trail and boardwalk passes through their preferred habitats of bottomland thickets and bald cypress swamps. Tall pines in higher areas and Spring Creek at the northern boundary add to the habitat diversity. Fox, gray, and flying squirrels are found in the park along with swamp rabbits, other small mammals, white-tailed deer, bobcats, and coyotes. Wood duck, pileated and other woodpeckers, red-shouldered hawk, barred owl, egrets and herons, and many songbirds live here. Look for water snakes and amphibians around ponds and along the canoe trail and for brown snakes and ground skinks on the forest floor.

Viewing Information: Large mammals are usually active at night and are rarely observed, except for deer. Most other featured species are frequently viewed, except flying squirrels, which also are nocturnal.

Directions: From Humble, north of Houston about nineteen miles on U.S. 59, go west on FM 1960 for 1.8 miles to Kenswick Drive. Turn north for one mile to park entrance.

Ownership: Harris County (713-446-8588)
Size: 225 acres
Closest Town: Humble

REGION 7: MOUNTAINS AND BASINS

Here is the classic western landscape: huge mountain ranges rising above desert valleys and grassy plateaus. Each of the eight major mountain ranges possesses its own set of animals and plants, and many rare species are found near desert springs, in canyons, and on mountaintops. Livestock grazing is the principal land use. Elevations vary from 2,500 to 8,749 feet at Guadalupe Peak. Annual rainfall ranges from eight to eighteen inches, the lowest levels in Texas.

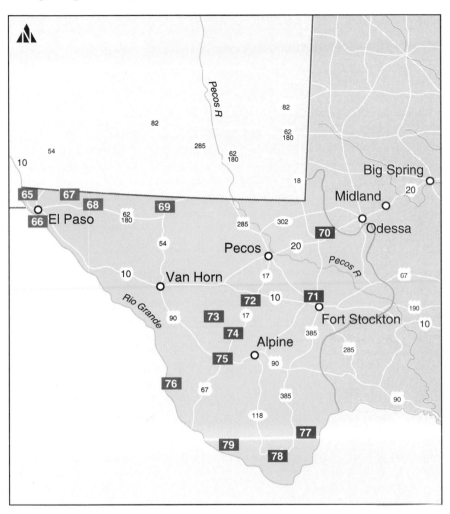

65	Franklin Mountains State Park	74	Davis Mountains State Park
66	Feather Lake Wildlife Sanctuary	75	Marfa Area
67	Hueco Tanks State HistoricalPark	76	Ocotillo Unit/Las Palomas
68	Hueco Mountains/Cornudas Drive		Wildlife Management Area
69	Guadalupe Mountains National Park	77	Black Gap Wildlife
70	Manahans Sandhills State park		Management Area
71	Diamond Y Springs Preserve	78	Big Bend National Park
72	Balmorhea State Park	79	Big Bend Ranch State
73	Davis Mountains Scenic Drive		Natural Area

65 FRANKLIN MOUNTAINS STATE PARK

Description: Stark beauty, isolation, hidden spring oases, secretive wildlife, and desert plants characterize this site. In the canyons, mule deer, gray fox, coyote, and ringtail can occasionally be seen very early or late in the day. Wildlife is more abundant near permanent water, such as in Whispering Springs Canyon or West Cottonwood Springs Canyon, where residents include porcupine, ground and rock squirrels, bats, cottontails and black-tailed jackrabbits, Gambel's quail, hummingbirds, numerous warblers, black-throated sparrow, blue grosbeak, flycatchers, and Scott's oriole. Five species of wrens sing in these canyons as red-tailed hawk, common raven, white-throated swift, and violet-green swallow soar overhead. Lizards are abundant, and snakes, including rattlesnakes, are occasionally viewed during warm months.

Viewing Information: Viewing probability is high for small mammals and reptiles during the summer and for ravens, hawks, and songbirds from spring through early fall, especially near springs. Large mammals are rarely viewed. Bats may be seen just before dark during the summer. Please exercise care when visiting springs because these habitats are fragile.

Directions: From Interstate 10 in El Paso, drive north on the North/South Freeway for 8.5 miles to Trans-Mountain/Loop 375 exit. Proceed west on the Trans-Mountain Road for three miles to a small parking area and trail entrance to Whispering Springs Canyon. Obtain permission to visit the spring from Fort Bliss (915-568-7930). Go west for 4.1 miles and turn north for one mile to the old Tom Mays Park, turn east on rocky road for .5 mile to a gate. Hike to West Cottonwood Springs Canyon and other wilderness areas from this point.

Ownership: TPWD (915-877-1528)
Size: 23,000 acres
Closest Town: El Paso

The Franklin Mountains attract individuals inspired by the stark beauty and isolation of the West. Very early or late hours are excellent times to experience this site, but don't neglect mid-day and night, because the mood, as well as the wildlife viewing, changes with the hour. LAURENCE PARENT

Description: An excellent urban site for migrant and wintering waterfowl such as cinnamon teal and common merganser, migrant shorebirds, great blue and other herons, egrets, white-faced ibis, and songbirds like the abundant red-winged blackbird in the marsh plants and surrounding trees.

Viewing Information: Viewing is likely for species in each group.

Directions: Take Interstate 10 about seventeen miles southeast from downtown El Paso and turn south at the Avenue of the Americas exit. After about 1.5 mile, turn west on North Loop Road (FM 76) for less than a mile to sanctuary on left. Open October through April, 3:30 p.m. to dusk each Sunday and from 8:00 a.m. to 11:00 a.m. on the first and third Saturday of each month. Visits at other times can be arranged through the El Paso Audubon Society.

Ownership: El Paso (El Paso/Trans-Pecos Audubon Society, 915-852-3119)
Size: 43.5 acres
Closest Town: El Paso

Loss of habitat is the principle threat to wildlife populations and Texas has lost significant amounts of many types. For instance, 98% of the original blackland prairie, 63% of the bottomland hardwoods, and at least 35% of the coastal marshes, have been lost.

67 HUECO TANKS STATE HISTORICAL PARK

Description: Huge rock islands and diverse wildlife, two features not usually associated, characterize this unique park. The link is water. Springs and seeps around the rocks provide permanent water while shallow depressions in the rocks, known as *huecos* collect rainfall. Juniper, oaks, and other trees, combined with water and shelter, attract bobcat, gray fox, ringtails, an occasional mountain lion, skunks, mule deer, cottontails and black-tailed jackrabbits. Over 200 species of birds are recorded including many rare migrating warblers. Hundreds of white-throated swifts and violet-green swallows whoosh around steep cliffs past red-tailed hawks and the uncommon golden eagle. In winter, look for mountain chickadee, mountain and western bluebirds, lark bunting, and prairie falcon. Snakes and lizards are abundant. Of particular interest are the fairy, tadpole, and clam shrimp that thrive when the huecos hold water. The park is famous for Native American pictographs.

Viewing Information: Although mountain lion and bobcat are rarely seen, their scat can be found in remote parts of the park. Viewing probability is high for small mammals all year, swifts and other nesting birds from spring through early fall, chickadee and bluebirds in winter, and shrimp during warm periods when huecos hold water. Probability is moderate for other featured species.

Directions: *Drive about thirty-two miles east of El Paso on U.S. 62-180 to RR 2775, then north about six miles to the park.*

Ownership: TPWD (915-857-1135)
Size: 860 acres
Closest Town: El Paso

Description: A beautiful drive through rocky mountains and grasslands. Look for mule deer and golden eagles during a fifteen-mile drive through the Hueco mountains. Pronghorn antelope are more abundant on the east side of the mountains where grassland is more extensive. A large prairie dog town with a few burrowing owls is scattered along the road in grasslands. Black-tailed jack-rabbits can be numerous at night.

Viewing Information: Viewing probability for pronghorn antelope and prairie dogs is high. It is low for mule deer and golden eagles, but best for deer in the mountains early or late in the day. Watch animals only from roadside because adjacent land is privately owned and trespassing is not allowed. Use caution when parking on side of road. No facilities at this site.

Directions: Drive about thirty-five miles east of El Paso on U.S. 62-180 to Hueco Mountains, just east of RR 2775. Prairie dog town is about nine miles west of Cornudas.

Ownership: State Department of Transportation (915-778-4254)
Size: Approximately thirty miles
Closest Town: Cornudas

With its amazing speed, excellent vision, and ability to exist without water for long periods, the pronghorn antelope is well-adapted to life on the plains. Pronghorn populations were drastically reduced in 1924 by changes in land use practices and over-hunting, but have recovered with better management in recent years.

WENDY SHATTIL/BOB ROZINSKI

69 GUADALUPE MOUNTAINS NATIONAL PARK

Description: With elk, Rocky Mountain birds, rainbow trout, and forests of ponderosa pine and Douglas fir, this exceptionally beautiful park offers unique biological diversity and wildlife viewing opportunities. This exposed part of an ancient reef includes the five highest peaks in Texas, as well as diverse habitats—playa lakes, sand dunes, Chihuahuan desert, grasslands, oak savannahs, pinyon/juniper forests, mixed conifer forests, and alpine meadows. Steep-walled canyons carved by permanent streams are lined with pines in the high country and maples at lower elevations. Mule deer, desert and gray foxes, black bear, mountain lion, coyote, ringtail, bats, porcupine, cottontails and black-tailed jackrabbit, antelope squirrel, wood rats, and rock squirrel are viewed here. Mountain lion and black bear are present but infrequently seen. Three species—the red squirrel, gray-footed chipmunk (the only chipmunk in Texas), and Mexican vole—occur nowhere else in the state. Watch for beautiful Steller's jay, mountain chickadee, pygmy nuthatch, western bluebird, broad-tailed hummingbird, band-tailed pigeon, white-throated swift, and red crossbills, as well as gray vireos, western tanagers, and acorn woodpeckers. Golden eagles and peregrine falcons are occasionally seen. Less commonly observed northern species are spotted owl in pine canyons and the Bowl, Clark's nutcracker in the highlands, and pinyon jay in pinyon/juniper woodlands. About 290 species of birds and fifty-five species of reptiles and amphibians are found in the park.

Viewing Information: Mule deer and, less frequently, elk are observed along the roads leading to Pine Springs, Frijole Ranch, and McKittrick Canyon. Elk are occasionally seen in the Bowl at about 8,000 feet. Although there are no roads into the park interior, more than eighty miles of rugged, steep hiking trails lead into the backcountry. McKittrick Canyon and the Bowl are productive viewing areas. Viewing probability is low for falcons, eagles, spotted owls, and large mammals other than deer. Small numbers of Clark's nutcracker and pinyon jay are present some years. The red squirrel is rare, but chipmunks are easily viewed near trees in the highlands. The vole is restricted to mountain meadows where it can be seen scurrying down tiny runways through grass near logs. The other featured species also are easily observed, except for gray vireos and red crossbills. Rainbow trout are commonly seen in McKittrick Creek just below the point where the trail climbs steeply.

Directions: *The park is 110 miles east of El Paso and fifty-five miles southwest of Carlsbad, New Mexico, on U.S. 62-180. Detailed maps of the park are available from the information center, which is on U.S. 62-180 about nine miles north of the junction of U.S. 62-180 and Texas 54.*

Ownership: NPS (915-828-3251)
Size: 86,415 acres
Closest Town: Carlsbad, New Mexico

Guadalupe Mountains National Park features the highest mountain in Texas, an 8,749 foot-high peak, and many other beautiful high-elevation vistas. The diverse plant and animal life is reminiscent of the Rocky Mountains to the north.

LAURENCE PARENT

70 **MONAHANS SANDHILLS STATE PARK**

Description: Tracks in the sand offer interesting insights about the behavior and ecology of animals that are seldom seen. Coyote and skunk tracks in the morning tell about nighttime visits to picnic areas. Bobcat and jackrabbit tracks in one area, roadrunner and lizard tracks in another, document life-and-death chases across the dunes. Mule deer prints indicate which plants were recently eaten. A pack rat trail leads to a large nest of wood and other plant material. Insect diversity is revealed by variation in numerous small trails. These animals, owls, songbirds, and many others also can be occasionally seen from the visitor center or while hiking through the park. An unusual tree, the shin oak, grows only two to four feet tall, produces huge acorns, and has a root system long enough to reach water from the tops of dunes up to seventy feet in height, which helps stabilize the dunes.

Viewing Information: The probability of finding tracks is very high, especially in the early morning. Viewing probability is high for small mammals and birds but low for large mammals.

Directions: *The park is off Interstate 20 about thirty miles west of Odessa or six miles east of Monahans.*

Ownership: TPWD (915-943-2092)
Size: 3,840 acres
Closest Town: Monahans

Dramas of nature are frequently told in the sand. For instance, a trail of a beetle as it was caught by a lizard, the K-shaped prints of a roadrunner following lizard tracks until the lizard disappeared, or prints on a nearby dune where coyotes howled earlier. RALPH LEE HOPKINS

Description: Comanche Springs in Fort Stockton was once one of the largest springs in Texas, gushing at a rate of thirty-five million gallons a day. It and several other large springs are now dry, leaving Diamond Y Springs as one of the last flowing springs and marsh communities in the region. This uncommon community is habitat for three rare snails, an unusual species of plant, and six native fish, including two endangered species, the Leon Springs pupfish and the Pecos mosquito fish. Surrounding marshes are good for viewing wildflowers, songbirds, and red-tailed hawks. The puzzle sunflower, a rare salt-tolerant species, blooms in mid to late summer.

Viewing Information: Visits to this site must be guided by the site manager and arranged in advance. The chances of viewing the fish, hawks, songbirds, and wildflowers are very good. No facilities at this site.

Directions: Visitors should call the Texas Nature Conservancy at the number below to arrange tours of the springs and obtain directions to the site.

Ownership: Texas Nature Conservancy (915-336-7615)
Size: 1,502 acres
Closest Town: Fort Stockton

Green in the desert means water, and water means fish and other wildlife. This oasis is produced by the Diamond Y Springs, seen near the center of this photo. It is home to several endangered and rare fish.

THE TEXAS NATURE
CONSERVANCY

72 BALMORHEA STATE PARK

Description: Scuba divers, snorkelers, swimmers, and walk-in visitors will find an exceptional wildlife viewing opportunity at the world's largest spring-fed swimming pool. San Solomon Springs gushes out 26 million gallons of crystal clear water each day into the concrete-rimmed pool with an eighty-foot visibility and a constant temperature of about seventy-five degrees. Ten species of fish are recorded including the familiar green sunfish, channel catfish, and largemouth bass. Thousands of three-inch, silvery Mexican tetras swarm around divers. Two endangered species of fish, although present in the pool, are more abundant and visible in the adjoining canals where swimming is prohibited. The Comanche Springs pupfish has a stocky, golden, two-inch body, mottled on the sides, and hides among the shallow, grassy parts of the canals and pool. The Pecos mosquito fish, 1.5 inches long or less, resembles a golden minnow, and also hides in the grass. Crayfish, soft-shell turtles, and several rare aquatic snails also live in the pool. Bird watching is good at the site and nearby Lake Balmorhea.

Viewing Information: The tetra, pupfish, and green sunfish are easily viewed in the pool. Viewing probability also is high for the mosquito fish, pupfish, and snails in the canals. The other featured species are either less common or, as with the turtle and crayfish, active at night. Divers should note that no compressed air is available within 100 miles. Diving hours are from 8:30 a.m. to 11:30 a.m. in the summer and until 8:00 p.m. the rest of the year.

Directions: Take Interstate 10 west past Fort Stockton to U.S. 290. The park is four miles southwest of the town of Balmorhea on U.S. 290.

Ownership: TPWD (915-375-2370)
Size: Fifty acres
Closest Town: Balmorhea

The pool and canals at Balmorhea State Park provide unique viewing opportunities for mexican tetras (shown here), as well as two species of endangered desert fishes, and several other native fishes. Bird watching is also very good in the area. STEPHAN MYERS

Description: One of the most scenic and perhaps the most productive wildlife viewing tours in the state. Golden eagles, prairie falcons, common black-hawks, gray fox, and coyotes should be looked for anywhere along the drive. Watch for Montezuma quail, mule deer, pinyon jay, and Clark's nutcracker in the pinyon pine-juniper-oak woodland and savannahs. Riparian woodlands, such as near the Madera Canyon Picnic Area, should be searched for wood-peckers, including Lewis' woodpecker with its crowlike flight, and songbirds, especially warblers during spring and fall migrations. Also watch for raccoons, skunks, and other small mammals. Pronghorn antelope, ferruginous hawks, longspurs, sparrows, and the unique mountain short-horned lizard are viewed in the grasslands to the west and south.

Viewing Information: Mammals can be seen all year and viewing probability is high for all but carnivores. Raptor viewing is best in winter, which also is the season to see longspurs and the uncommon pinyon jay, nutcracker, and woodpecker. Songbird viewing is good all year but best during migration. Viewing probability for the horned lizard is low to moderate during warm months. Most of the surrounding land is private and should not be entered without permission. Use caution when parking on roadside.

Directions: From Fort Davis, drive north on Texas 118 about thirty miles passing the McDonald Observatory and Madera Canyon Picnic Area, then take Texas 166 south past Sawtooth Mountain and the grasslands back to Fort Davis.

Ownership: Texas Department of Transportation (TPWD, 915-426-3337)
Size: Seventy-four miles
Closest Town: Fort Davis

Mountains of clouds framing mountains of rock are often seen on this spectacular scenic drive, which also passes through captivating grasslands. Plan enough time for a slow drive, then do it again at dusk or at night to see the most wildlife.
RALPH LEE HOPKINS

74 DAVIS MOUNTAINS STATE PARK

Description: Interesting and watchable wildlife, beautiful scenery, pleasant climate, and comfortable accommodations distinguish this site. Mule deer, javelina, gray fox, skunks, rock squirrel, red-tailed hawk, scrub jay, Cassin's kingbird, curve-billed thrasher, pyrrhuloxia, and black-headed grosbeak can be viewed from roads through the camp or along Skyline Drive, which leads to a scenic overlook. Montezuma quail is seen regularly around the camping area and its quavering song, like that of a whiny owl, intrigues the listener. This also is one of the few places where all three bluebirds occur. During severe winters, high-elevation species such as Steller's jay, mountain chickadee, and Townsend's solitaire move down into the park. A mixture of desert and high-elevation plants provides diverse wildflower viewing.

Viewing Information: Viewing probability is high for all but the high-elevation species. The kingbird and grosbeak are migratory. Javelina, fox, and skunk are most often seen at night. There are a number of trails, one of which connects with the Fort Davis National Historic Site.

Directions: *Entrance is four miles northwest of Fort Davis on Texas 118.*

Ownership: TPWD (915-426-3337)
Size: 2,350 acres
Closest Town: Fort Davis

Birdwatchers from around the world come to this park to see Montezuma quail. Occaisionally seen near water in the campground area, these birds are more often heard. Their unusual, owl-like call is difficult to localize but wonderful to experience. GLEN MILLS/TEXAS PARKS AND WILDLIFE DEPT.

75 MARFA AREA

Description: Pronghorn antelope are reliably viewed in grasslands along the first fifteen miles of any highway leaving Marfa. Coyotes, black-tailed jackrabbits, and grassland birds are also commonly observed. Fields one mile south of town on the east side of U.S. 67 are particularly productive. When flooded, these fields attract wading birds, waterfowl from fall to early spring, and shorebirds in early spring and mid-summer.

Viewing Information: Viewing probability is high during the day for pronghorn antelope. Coyotes and rabbits are most active at night but can be seen early and late in the day. Property beyond the road is private and should not be entered. Use caution when parking on roadside. No facilities at this site.

Directions: *Marfa is about eighty-eight miles southwest of Fort Stockton. To drive to Marfa from Interstate 10, take U.S. 67 from the east, U.S. 90 from the west, or Texas 17 from the north.*

Ownership: Texas Department of Transportation (TPWD, 915-837-2051)
Size: About seventy-five miles
Closest Town: Marfa

76 OCOTILLO UNIT—LAS PALOMAS WILDLIFE MANAGEMENT AREA

Description: Early morning sounds of white-winged doves cooing and Gambel's quail singing coupled with the rattles and squawks of yellow-breasted chats make the effort to drive here worthwhile. A mixture of desert and river habitats attracts a surprising abundance and diversity of wildlife. Look for Harris' hawk, waterfowl, wading birds, black-chinned hummingbird, Scott's oriole, vermillion flycatcher, Lucy's warbler, and varied buntings. Lizards and snakes are abundant.

Viewing Information: Viewing probability is high for featured species except javelina, which are more active at night, and the rare Lucy's warbler. Drive carefully on Farm Road 170 because livestock roam freely, the road undulates like a roller coaster, and flash floods are common during rain. The site is remote; bring your own supplies, including water. Wildlife viewing may be discouraged during the hunting season. Registration at the headquarters in Alpine, and a Texas Conservation Passport are required for entry.

Directions: *Entrance is thirty-six miles northwest of Presidio and one mile north of Ruidosa on FM 170. Site map is available at headquarters.*

Ownership: TPWD (915-837-2051)
Size: 2,082 acres   **Closest Town:** Presidio

77 BLACK GAP WILDLIFE MANAGEMENT AREA

Description: Rugged wilderness, arid mountains, and distinct wildlife characterize this wildlife management area, the largest in Texas. Over 260 species of birds recorded here include bald and golden eagles, sixteen species of ducks and geese, seven hummingbirds, and many warblers. Bobcats, coyotes, and a few black bear occur on the site. Reptiles are diverse and abundant, including at least three species of large rattlesnakes, beautiful "red racers," common round-tailed horned lizards, collared lizards, and several species of whiptails. Tamaulipan desert scrub and Chihuahuan desert plant communities meet here contributing to the overall diversity.

Viewing Information: Most of the backcountry roads require a four-wheel-drive. Viewing probability from the roads is moderate to high for deer, javelina, skunks, reptiles, and amphibians but low for badgers, ringtail, and kit foxes during early morning, late afternoon, and at night. During the day, look for mammal signs, hawks, ground squirrels, snakes, and lizards. Sitting quietly by water tanks or rafting the Rio Grande along the southern border through the canyons can yield exceptional views of a variety of wildlife, especially songbirds. Wildlife viewing may be discouraged during the hunting season. Bring plenty of water because the site is remote. Use extreme caution in the backcountry and avoid flash flood areas. Registration at headquarters and a Texas Conservation Passport are required.

Directions: *Drive south from Fort Stockton on U.S. 385 for ninety-seven miles, turn southeast on FM 2627 for eighteen miles to headquarters.*

Ownership: TPWD (915-837-2051)
Size: 102,000 acres   **Closest Town:** Marathon

The coyote is widespread in Texas where it is the most frequently viewed large carnivore. Their calls, indicative of the wild to some people, start out as a solo performance, become a chorus and increase in volume, usually ending in a mournful squall.
JEFF FOOTT

Description: One of the world's premier wildlife viewing areas, this park hosts almost eighty species of mammals, over 400 species of birds, fifty-six species of reptiles including thirty kinds of snakes. Many animals such as the Colima warbler, greater long-nosed bat, and Carmen Mountains white-tailed deer are not found anywhere else north of Mexico. The endangered Big Bend mosquito fish occurs nowhere else on earth. Big Bend offers the highest probability in Texas of viewing black bear and mountain lions.

The Chisos Mountains function as a green island in a desert sea, harboring relict populations of species such as ponderosa pine, Douglas-fir, and quaking aspen, typical of more northern mountains, and the Texas madrone, a beautiful red-barked tree with tropical relatives. A narrow band of grasslands near the base of the mountains is surrounded by the Chihuahuan Desert, known for its beautiful wildflower displays. The Rio Grande cuts through the mountains and deserts, forming a linear oasis rich in wildlife.

Viewing Information: Over 150 miles of hiking trails traverse the park. The patient observer has a good chance of viewing the Colima warbler along several of the high-country trails in the late spring and summer. The probability of seeing many of the other songbirds and butterflies is high during the spring and fall migrations at the Rio Grande Village, Chisos Basin, mountain canyons, and desert springs. Golden eagles and peregrine falcons nest in the park but are not easily seen. Fourteen hummingbird species, plus band-tailed pigeons, white-throated swifts, flycatchers, and Scott's orioles can be observed feeding on summer blossoms of century plants. At night, the quiet observer can hear the whooshing of greater long-nosed bats as they fly around these plants pollinating the flowers. The steep drive from Panther Junction through Green Gulch to Chisos Basin offers the best probabilities for viewing white-tailed deer and collared peccary, which are common, as well as uncommon species like black bear and mountain lion. Mule deer are seen at the lower elevations. "Red racers," a pink variation of the western coachwhip, and bullsnakes are frequently seen on roads and trails during summer days. Use caution driving the roads and when slowing down or parking to view wildlife. Many backcountry roads require off-road vehicles.

Directions: *From the east, drive south from Fort Stockton on U.S. 385 for 126 miles to park headquarters at Panther Junction. From the west, drive southeast on U.S. 90 from Van Horn for 100 miles to Alpine, turn south for seventy-eight miles on Texas 118 to Study Butte, then east on Texas 118 for twenty-six miles to Panther Junction.*

Ownership: NPS (915-477-2251)
Size: 801,163 acres   **Closest Town:** Study Butte

The mountain lion, sometimes known as cougar or puma, is the largest native cat left in Texas. This lion, as well as black bear, are most frequently (but still rarely) seen in Big Bend National Park, previous page. Check with rangers about precautions to use when hiking in mountain lion country. DENNIS HENRY

A large part of the great biological diversity of this national park is associated with the high habitat diversity: from the river and its forests through the desert and grasslands, and up the mountain to ponderosa pine and Douglas fir forests and meadows. LAURENCE PARENT

Description: Spectacular landscapes and a harsh desert climate, coupled with the life-giving Rio Grande and spring-nurtured oases called *cienagas*, have created habitats for this exceptional wildlife community. Almost 400 species of birds occur in the area, including many raptors, hummingbirds, and warblers as well as desert forms like the cactus wren, pyrrhuloxia, and black-throated sparrow. Large mammals include coyotes, a population of mule deer, and javelina, the principal prey for resident mountain lions. Western pipistrelles and western mastiff bats, which are the smallest and largest bats respectively in the United States, are seen and heard in the canyons. Desert-adapted species, like the kangaroo rat and spiny lizards, are common. During wet years the Chihuahuan Desert grassland springs to life with lush grasses and wildflowers. Insects, including monarch butterflies during migration and the large horse lubber grasshoppers, can become very abundant.

Viewing Information: During the migratory and nesting seasons, zone-tailed hawks, golden eagles, and peregrine falcons occasionally soar over the ranch, and violet-green swallows and white-throated swifts frequently swoop around the steep-walled canyons along the scenic sixty-mile drive from Lajitas to Presidio. Migrant songbirds, such as hermit's and Townsend's warblers, are sometimes present but seldom abundant in trees by the river and near the *cienagas* along the thirty-mile Rancherias Loop Trail. Although mountain lions are uncommon and usually detected by their signs, deer, javelina, coyotes, and reptiles can be regularly viewed from Farm Road 170 and while on the bus tour into the backcountry. Check the tour schedules and pay entrance fees at the Warnock Center or Fort Leaton, which also offer interpretive materials, botanical walks, and wildlife viewing opportunities. A careful drive along Farm Road 170 at night offers a slim chance of seeing a desert fox or badger and a good chance of seeing reptiles, amphibians, and bats. Be prepared for hiking in the desert, which can be harsh, and always be aware of flash floods.

Directions: *From the east, drive south from Interstate 10 on U.S. 67 for forty-eight miles, turn nine miles west on U.S. 90 to Alpine, then seventy-eight miles south to Study Butte. Turn west on FM 170 for twelve miles to the Warnock Environmental Education Center, one mile east of Lajitas. From the west, drive southeast on U.S. 90 from Van Horn for seventy-four miles to Marfa, turn south for sixty-one miles on U.S. 67 to Presidio, then southeast on FM 170 for four miles to Fort Leaton State Park.*

Ownership: TPWD (915-424-3327)
Size: 263,897 acres
Closest Town: Lajitas

Collared peccary, or javelina as it is often called, can usually be seen in the early morning or just before dusk. Contrary to popular opinion, javelina seldom attack people or root in the ground. They eat a great deal of cacti, especially prickly pear, which provides water as well as nutrition. EARL NOTTINGHAM

REGION 8: HILL COUNTRY

This is a land of many springs, stony hills with broad divides, and steep drainages. The limestone of the Edwards Plateau is honeycombed with thousands of caves, some of which contain large colonies of Mexican free-tailed bats. Other cave-dwellers such as blind catfish and blind salamanders are now endangered, as human demand for water depletes the Edwards Aquifer faster than it can be replenished. Endangered golden-cheeked warblers and black-capped vireos can be seen in the Ashe juniper/oak forests of this region. Elevations range from 1,200 to 3,000 feet; annual rainfall varies from twelve to thirty-two inches.

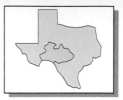

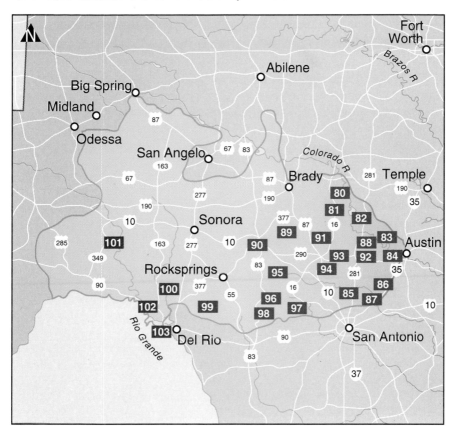

80	Colorado Bend State Park	93	Lyndon B. Johnson State Historical Park
81	Lake Buchanan	94	Old Tunnel Wildlife Management Area
82	Inks Lake State Park		
83	Lake Travis Area	95	Kerr Wildlife Management Area
84	Austin Area	96	Lost Maples State Natural Area
85	Guadalupe River State Park/Honey Creek State Natural Area	97	Hill Country State Natural Area
		98	Garner State Park
86	San Marcos Springs	99	Kickapoo Caverns State Park
87	Comal Springs/Landa Park	100	Devils River State Natural Area
88	Hamilton Pool/Westcave Preserve	101	Chandler Independence Creek Preserve
89	Eckert James River Bat Cave		
90	South Llano State Park/ Walter Buck Wildlife Management Area	102	Seminole Canyon State Historical Park
91	Enchanted Rock State Natural Area	103	Amistad National Recreation Area
92	Pedernales Falls State Park		

80 COLORADO BEND STATE PARK

Description: An attractive park featuring the endangered golden-cheeked warbler and black-capped vireo, white-tailed deer, Guadalupe bass (the state fish of Texas), and cave-adapted animals. The upland savannahs, river woodlands, the Colorado River, and streams attract bald eagles, hawks, abundant songbirds, and others.

Viewing Information: The portion of the park where most of the endangered species are found is sensitive to disturbance and has restricted visitation. Guided tours of this area and Gorman Cave can be arranged through park headquarters. Viewing probability is moderate for the endangered birds from April through June and eagles during the winter, high for other species.

Directions: *From Lampasas at the intersection of U.S. 183 and U.S. 281, take FM 580 about twenty-four miles west to Bend. Follow signs on an unpaved road for six miles south of Bend to park entrance.*

Ownership: TPWD (512-628-3240) **Size:** 5,328 acres **Closest Town:** Bend

81 LAKE BUCHANAN

Description: An excellent site for bald eagles, osprey, cormorants, red-breasted mergansers and many other species of ducks, common loons, horned grebes, Bonaparte's gulls and other marine birds, great blue herons, and king-fishers. White-tailed deer, small mammals, and numerous songbirds on land.

Viewing Information: Viewing probability for eagles, osprey, and waterfowl is high from a boat in winter. Privately owned Vanishing Texas River Cruise (512-756-6986) conducts comfortable tours for a fee to see waterfalls, eagles, and other wildlife. Reservations are recommended. Viewing of land species is moderate to high. Cedar Point Resource Area offers good viewing of land species and shoreline viewing of aquatic species.

Directions: *The eagle cruise departs from a dock reached by driving west of Burnet for three miles on Texas 29, then north on FM 2341 for 13.5 miles to entrance. To reach Cedar Point, near the community of Tow, drive east of Llano for about two miles on Texas 29, then northeast on FM 2241 to Bluffton. Continue north on FM 2241 for about four miles and turn east on FM 3014 to site entrance.*

Ownership: LCRA (512-473-4083) **Size:** 23,500 acres **Closest Town:** Burnet

82 INKS LAKE STATE PARK

Description: One of the best sites to view white-tailed deer and wild turkey. Breeding songbirds include cactus wren, verdin, black-throated sparrow, orchard oriole, the endangered black-capped vireo, and many others. Bald eagles and numerous species of waterfowl winter on the lake. Colorful lizards and snakes occupy the rocky outcrops and hills. Channel catfish and endangered paddlefish can be viewed at the U.S. Fish Hatchery, also an excellent site for waterfowl.

Viewing Information: Viewing probability is high for deer, turkey, and many songbirds while hiking the 7.5 miles of trails or at campsites. The black-capped vireo is frequently seen and heard from April to August. Eagles are infrequently observed as are osprey during spring and fall migrations, which is when songbirds are also most diverse. Fish are easily seen at the hatchery. Reptiles are most abundant in summer.

Directions: Inks Lake State Park is nine miles west of Burnet on Texas 29, then three miles south on PR 4. The fish hatchery is one mile south of the park on PR 4.

Ownership: TPWD (512-793-2223) **Size:** 1,200 acres **Closest Town:** Burnet

83 LAKE TRAVIS AREA

Description: Featured species include the endangered black-capped vireo and golden-cheeked warbler, as well as waterfowl, red-tailed hawks and other raptors, wild turkeys, great blue herons and other wading birds, other songbirds, white-tailed deer, armadillos, and other small mammals.

Viewing Information: Viewing probability is high for all but the endangered species, which can usually be viewed or heard with increased effort from April through July. Public sites include Travis County managed parks like Hippie Hollow, where black-capped vireos are seen near the parking area. Golden-cheeked warblers are predictable at Wheless Resource Area, one of three parks on the north shore, managed by the Lower Colorado River Authority.

Directions: To reach Pace Bend Park, take Texas 71 about twenty-seven miles west of Austin, then FM 2322 for 4.6 miles east to entrance. Hippie Hollow is on Comanche Trail, about 2.5 miles north of FM 620. Take RR 2222 north from Austin for about ten miles to FM 620, then west to Comanche Trail. Call LCRA for directions to its sites.

Ownership: LCRA (512-473-4083), Travis County (512-472-7483)
Size: 18,900 acres
Closest Town: Austin

84 AUSTIN AREA

Description: Austin is an exceptional urban wildlife viewing area. This capital city of Texas boasts the world's largest metropolitan bat colony, accessible populations of the endangered golden-cheeked warbler and black-capped vireo, wading birds, white-tailed deer, squirrels, butterfly gardens, clear streams, lakes, and beautiful scenery. Austin also contains numerous nature preserves and many acres of parks and greenbelts.

Viewing Information: From April until October, the probability is high for viewing about 750,000 Mexican free-tailed bats as they leave their roost under the Congress Avenue Bridge. It is moderate for deer all year and for the endangered birds between April and July in Emma Long Park, Barton Creek Greenbelt, and the Balcones Canyonlands Refuge and Bioreserve, which is being developed to protect habitats for seven endangered species. Songbird and insect viewing is very good in Wild Basin and Zilker Park with its botanical and butterfly gardens.

Directions: *Congress Avenue Bridge is downtown across Town Lake. Zilker Park and the Barton Creek Greenbelt are about a mile west of the bridge on Barton Springs Road. Wild Basin is on the west side of town off of Loop 360. Emma Long Park is just west of Loop 360 and six miles south of RR 2222. The bioreserve will include parts of Austin and some of the oak/juniper wildlands north to the county line.*

Ownership: Various (City of Austin, 512-499-6700; Wild Basin, 512-327-7622) **Size:** Various
Closest Town: Austin

Hundreds of wildlife watchers from around the world travel to Hill Country each year to view black-capped vireos (pictured here) and golden-cheeked warblers. Both birds are included on the state and federal lists of endangered species. The breeding habitats of these neotropical migrants are restricted to Texas.
GREG W. LASLEY

Description: A picturesque park of rugged cliffs along the impressive Guadalupe River. Look for cliff swallows, the Guadalupe bass, mallards, turtles, abundant deer and turkey, soaring raptors, and singing songbirds. Also featured are the endangered golden-cheeked warblers, which nest only in the unique combination of Ashe juniper and oak covering some slopes and canyons in the hill country. Wildflowers are best viewed in the natural area.

Viewing Information: The chances of seeing the warbler are good from April through June. Although bass can be viewed from the bank, they are more easily observed from a canoe or tube while running the rapids in the river. Other species are easily viewed, but swallows migrate south in the fall. Visitation to the natural area is by guided tours each Saturday morning.

Directions: Take U.S. 281 north from San Antonio for about thirty miles, then Texas 46 west for eight miles to PR 31, then north three miles.

Ownership: TPWD (512-438-2656)
Size: 1,940 acres, 2,294 acres in natural area **Closest Town:** Bulverde

Guadalupe bass, the state fish of Texas, is known as a "Texas specialty," found only in the river systems of Hill Country. Patient wildlife watchers can see this distinctive fish swimming among the rocks and holes in clear waters of the region.

DR. GARY P. GARRETT/TEXAS PARKS AND WILDLIFE DEPARTMENT

86 SAN MARCOS SPRINGS

Description: From glass-bottomed boats, visitors can see schools of native fish and the large springs that create Spring Lake and the San Marcos River. Large blue catfish, including a few introduced albinos, beautiful Rio Grande perch, the popular largemouth bass, and several exotic fish are some of the species that can be observed. The endangered San Marcos salamander and fountain darter as well as several species of turtles also are present. Small amounts of an endangered species of native rice are present in shallow, fast-flowing parts of the river below the lake. Songbirds are abundant in trees around the river, especially from March through June.

Viewing Information: The springs are in a private resort and amusement park called Aquarena Springs, which operates the glass-bottomed boats. Viewing is excellent for all but the endangered wildlife, which are difficult to see.

Directions: Take the Aquarena Springs Drive west from Interstate 35 in San Marcos and follow signs to the resort and amusement park.

Ownership: Aquarena Springs Resort and Conference Center (512-396-8900)
Size: Ninety acres
Closest Town: San Marcos

The Edward's Aquifer, an underground body of water in the hill country, has more species that exist beneath the ground for their entire lives that any other aquifer on earth. Many species, such as the Texas blind salamander and toothless blindcat (a catfish), are colorless and do not have eyes. This unique ecosystem could be lost unless we properly manage the use of its water.

Description: This is the largest freshwater spring in the southwest and is a unique ecosystem that includes aquatic insects found nowhere else in the world and two endangered species, the San Marcos salamander and the fountain darter, a reddish brown fish about one inch long. Numerous other fish, native and exotic, as well as crayfish and turtles can be viewed in the stream. Mallards and other waterfowl, great blue heron and other wading birds, and nutria occur in the stream.

Viewing Information: Observations of the endangered species are very difficult since they prefer vegetated stream bottoms and mats of green algae. Probability is low to moderate for viewing other featured species.

Directions: From Interstate 35 in New Braunfels, take Seguin Avenue northwest following signs to Landa Park Drive, which leads through the park to the springs.

Ownership: City of New Braunfels (512-629-7275)
Size: 196 acres
Closest Town: New Braunfels

More than just beautiful, Comal Springs are also the largest springs in Texas, and home to endangered salamanders, fish, and other animals. These unique springs may stop flowing by the year 2010 if water from the Edwards Aquifer, an underground lake, continues to be used faster than it is replenished by rainfall.
GARY L. GRAHAM

88 HAMILTON POOL AND WESTCAVE PRESERVE

Description: Diverse songbirds, abundant wildflowers, scenic waterfalls, sharp habitat contrasts, and lush vegetation are trademarks of these neighboring sites. Trails lead from upland savannahs and meadows down into moist, green, cool canyons that follow crystalline streams to beautiful waterfalls and caves. Some of the plants and birds, such as cypress trees and eastern phoebe, are typical of more eastern, wetter regions. Others, like mesquite and canyon wren, are near the edge of their western distribution. Several of the plants are endangered as are the golden-cheeked warblers at Westcave and bald eagles. Osprey, red-tailed hawks, white-tailed deer, and small mammals also are present. Large catfish and turtles can be seen swimming in pools beneath the waterfalls.

Viewing Information: Songbirds are abundant and easily viewed, especially during the spring and fall migrations. Viewing probability of golden-cheeked warblers is moderate at Westcave from April through July. Bald eagles and osprey are occasionally seen from a platform overlooking the Pedernales River at Westcave. Probability is high for viewing hawks, deer, fox squirrel, fish, and turtles. Visitation to Westcave is limited to guided tours, thirty people at a time, every two hours on weekends from 10:00 a.m. through 4:00 p.m. Group tours can be arranged on weekdays.

Directions: *Take Texas 71 west from Austin about eight miles to the community of Bee Cave. At the western edge of town, take FM 3238 west about thirteen miles to the entrance for Hamilton Pool. Continue west on FM 3238 for one mile to Westcave, which is the first gate on your right after crossing the Pedernales River bridge.*

Ownership: Travis Co. (Hamilton Pool, 512-264-2740), LCRA (Westcave, 512-825-3442)
Size: Westcave, thirty acres; Hamilton Pool, 230 acres
Closest Town: Bee Cave

Several species of wildlife in Texas have unusual mating systems. The males of both species of prairie chickens sing and dance to attract as many females as possible. Hummingbirds perform aerial acrobatics as part of their mating ritual. Little evening bats form harems in which a male lives with many females.

Hamilton Pool waterfall is one of the tallest and most beautiful in the state. The creek and steep-walled canyons here and at the nearby Westcave Preserve create moist habitats that contrast sharply with the dry surrounding areas. Such habitat diversity promotes high biological diversity. LAURENCE PARENT

89 | ECKERT JAMES RIVER BAT CAVE

Description: The smokelike column of five million Mexican free-tailed bats rising from their cave cast against the summer sun setting on picturesque wild country is one of nature's most awe-inspiring spectacles. White-tailed deer, black-tailed jackrabbit, cottontail rabbit, wild turkey, and red-tailed hawks can be seen along the road from the Llano River crossing to the James River crossing.

Viewing Information: Bats are reliably viewed from about an hour before dark (sometimes earlier, sometimes later) until well after dark from mid-May through mid-September. Viewing probability is high for deer, rabbits, turkey, and hawks. Please do not go beyond the viewing barrier and do not make loud noises because bats are easily disturbed. James River and several small creeks have to be driven through in order to reach the cave parking area. Use extreme caution when driving this road and crossing these creeks and river, especially during rain. The land on either side of the road is private and should not be trespassed to view wildlife or reach the river.

Directions: *From Mason on U.S. 87, go south on FM 1723 for 2.5 miles, then southwest on FM 2389 for about five miles to the Llano River. Turn right on the county road just past the river crossing and continue southwest for about eight miles to the James River. Drive through the water if it is not too high and for another mile to the parking area on the right.*

Ownership: Texas Nature Conservancy (512-224-8774)
Size: Ten acres   **Closest Town:** Mason

Huge granite rocks dominate the landscape of Enchanted Rock State Natural Area, attracting people today as they have for thousands of years. They also draw wildlife, including raptors that soar on the updrafts, and rock squirrels that scamper among the crevices. Trails to the top culminate in breathtaking vistas of Hill Country. STEPHAN MYERS

90 SOUTH LLANO STATE PARK AND WALTER BUCK WILDLIFE MANAGEMENT AREA

Description: Some of the most abundant and most easily viewed wild turkey and white-tailed deer populations in Texas coupled with outstanding river, bottomland, and hill country scenery make this new park and wildlife area one of the state's premier wildlife viewing sites. Watch for raccoon, ringtail, fox, bobcat, striped skunks, armadillo, beaver, fox and rock squirrels, eastern cottontail, wood duck, and great blue heron. Painted buntings, eastern bluebirds, endangered black-capped vireos, hummingbirds, and many other songbirds also are featured.

Viewing Information: Viewing probability is high for turkey, deer, armadillo, squirrels, rabbits, herons, and many songbirds. The probability is low for bobcat, ringtail, beaver, and the vireo and moderate for the other featured species. During winter, the wooded bottomland and river of the park is closed to visitors to protect a historic roost for as many as 500 turkeys. Wildlife viewing in the wildlife management area adjacent to the park may be discouraged during deer and turkey hunting seasons. Hunting blinds can be used as observation blinds during other times of the year.

Directions: Take U.S. 377 exit south from Interstate 10 to Junction, then five more miles on U.S. 377 to PR 73 and entrance.

Ownership: TPWD (512-446-3994)
Size: 2,630 acres **Closest Town:** Junction

91 ENCHANTED ROCK STATE NATURAL AREA

Description: Big beautiful granite rocks, lizards, white-tailed deer, wild turkey, soaring vultures and hawks, abundant small mammals, diverse songbirds, and sparkling creeks make this an especially attractive site to view wildlife.

Viewing Information: Hiking trails around and to the top of the rocks provide good viewing opportunities. Viewing probability is high for featured wildlife.

Directions: From Fredericksburg, drive eighteen miles north on FM 965 to entrance.

Ownership: TPWD (915-247-3903)
Size: 1,643 acres
Closest Town: Fredericksburg

92 PEDERNALES FALLS STATE PARK

Description: An excellent place to see wildlife and scenery typical of the hill country. The river and series of falls harbor green and belted kingfishers. Surrounding hills and canyons, covered with oaks and junipers, are home to endangered golden-cheeked warblers. Bewick's wren is found in the dryer uplands, Carolina wren along the river and streams, and canyon wren among rocky cliffs. Throughout the park, red-tailed hawks, turkey vultures, many songbirds, white-tailed deer, and wild turkeys are commonly viewed. At night, Chuck-will's widow can be heard from spring into summer and coyotes are sometimes seen.

Viewing Information: Probability is high for viewing or hearing featured species except the green kingfisher, which is uncommon, and the warbler, which is endangered. There is a moderately good chance of hearing and seeing the warbler from April through June on trails near bluffs along the river.

Directions: *West from Austin thirty-two miles on U.S. 290, then north six miles on FM 3232.*

Ownership: TPWD (512-868-7304)
Size: 4,860 acres
Closest Town: Johnson City

Moist canyons, with oak and Ashe juniper on the slopes, provide habitat for the endangered golden-cheeked warblers and other wildlife in Pedernales State Park. Hiking trails offer opportunities to experience habitats and view wildlife.
STEPHAN MYERS

Description: The best place in Texas to see and photograph bison in a natural setting. The bison have been reintroduced into the area. Red fox, white-tailed deer, armadillo, fox squirrel, cottontail rabbit, wild turkey, songbirds, and a nature trail with a hill country botanical exhibit also are featured. Additional exhibits reveal the interesting history of the region and the former president.

Viewing Information: All but the red fox, which is usually active at night, are easily viewed.

Directions: *The park is ten miles west of Johnson City on U.S. 290.*

Ownership: TPWD (512-644-2252)
Size: 700 acres
Closest Town: Stonewall

Small herds of bison, like the one at LBJ Historical Park, are reminders of what it must have been like to experience the thunderous sound of large herds running across open country. Overhunting, fences, railroads, and other land use practices contributed to the bison's disappearence from Texas by 1900. LARRY R. DITTO

94 OLD TUNNEL WILDLIFE MANAGEMENT AREA

Description: This is one of the easiest places for a family to experience a unique natural phenomenon as up to a million free-tailed bats fly in a meandering column backlit by spectacular sunsets, in one of the most beautiful parts of the hill country. Another bat, the cave myotis, is present but difficult to identify in flight. The historic railroad tunnel was abandoned in 1942 and the bats have been using the roost for at least twenty-five years. Roads to this roost are lined with picturesque farms. White-tailed deer are frequently seen along the roadside and songbirds abound in the forests at the end of the tunnel.

Viewing Information: Bats are reliably viewed from about an hour before dark (sometimes earlier, sometimes later) until well after dark from mid-April through mid-September. Please do not go beyond the viewing barrier and do not make loud noises because bats are easily disturbed. Reservations and a Texas Conservation Passport are required to visit this site.

Directions: *Drive two miles east of Fredericksburg to the Grapetown county road. Turn south and travel for eleven miles through Grapetown to the management area sign.*

Ownership: TPWD (512-896-2500)
Size: 10.5 acres   **Closest Town:** Fredericksburg

Most wildlife viewers stand in awe at the sight of Mexican free-tailed bats exiting their roost. The swirling, smoke-like column of bats can stretch for miles against the evening sky. LARRY R. DITTO

Description: This unusual and scenic wildlife management area has a self-guided driving tour to educate visitors about the relationships between wildlife and habitat changes due to different land-use practices. Viewable wildlife include the endangered golden-cheeked warbler and black-capped vireo, many other songbirds, gray fox, ringtail, raccoon, skunk, white-tailed deer, javelina, fox squirrel, and armadillo. Wild turkeys roost here in winter.

Viewing Information: The chances are good for viewing the endangered species from April through June. Deer, raccoon, skunk, and armadillo are seen all year. The chances are very good for squirrel, turkey, and many songbirds. They are poor for javelina, gray fox, and ringtail. Wildlife viewing may be discouraged during hunting seasons. Registration at area headquarters and a Texas Conservation Passport are required for entry. Deer are easier to see and camping is available at nearby Kerrville-Schreiner State Park.

Directions: *From Interstate 10, take Texas 16 south for two miles to Kerrville, then Texas 27 northwest to Ingram. Drive west on Texas 39 for about five miles to Hunt, then thirteen miles on FM 1340 to headquarters. The state park is three miles south of Kerrville on Texas 173.*

Ownership: TPWD (512-238-4483)
Size: 6,493 acres   **Closest Town:** Hunt

Six species of native cats are known from Texas but two, the jaguar and margay, are now extinct in the state. The only place in the United States where ocelots and jaguarundi survive is the rio Grande Valley of south Texas with its thick, subtropical habitats.

96 | LOST MAPLES STATE NATURAL AREA

Description: With over ten miles of trails through hills and canyons glowing in the fall with the reds and oranges of an isolated population of bigtooth maple, this is one of the most scenic hiking areas in Texas. Look for white-tailed deer, wild turkey, fox squirrel, golden eagle, red-tailed hawk, many songbirds, and three Texas specialties: golden-cheeked warbler, black-capped vireo, and green kingfisher. Springs and streams offer unique opportunities to see Guadalupe bass and green-throated darter, both unique to central Texas.

Viewing Information: Viewing probability is moderate to high for all featured species except the kingfisher, which is uncommon. The warbler and vireo are viewed from April through July. Reservations are recommended.

Directions: *From Interstate 10, take Texas 16 south for two miles to Kerrville, then Texas 27 west to Ingram. Drive west on Texas 39 for about twenty-seven miles to FM 187, then fourteen miles south on 187 to the park entrance.*

Ownership: TPWD (512-966-3413)
Size: 2,208 acres   **Closest Town:** Vanderpool

Autumn colors are just one attraction for Hill Country visitors. The state parks and natural areas protect a large part of the tremendous visual and biological diversity of the region, while offering opportunities to appreciate these areas through hiking and wildlife viewing. LAURENCE PARENT

97 HILL COUNTRY STATE NATURAL AREA

Description: With assorted wildlife, extensive grasslands, juniper and oak covered hillsides, rocky streams, an extensive network of hiking and equestrian trails, and scenic vistas, this site offers hill country at its best. Featured are white-tailed deer, skunks, ringtails, raccoons, squirrels, rabbits, armadillos, red-tailed and Swainson's hawks, wild turkeys, chuck-will's widow, and a multitude of songbirds, including the endangered golden-cheeked warbler and black-capped vireo. Lizards are numerous and wildflowers are diverse.

Viewing Information: Viewing probability is moderate for most featured wildlife species because they are either nocturnal or uncommon. Deer, red-tailed hawk, turkey, and many songbirds are frequently observed. Birds and flowers are most diverse in the spring.

Directions: *From Boerne on Interstate 10, take Texas 46 west for eleven miles, then Texas 16 west twelve miles to Bandera. Turn south on Texas 173 for one mile, then west on FM 1077 ten miles to entrance. Reservations required.*

Ownership: TPWD (512-796-4413)
Size: 5,370 acres
Closest Town: Bandera

98 GARNER STATE PARK

Description: Famous for spectacular scenery and cool, clear streams, this park also offers abundant wildlife. White-tailed deer, armadillo, and wild turkey can be seen all year. Also look for such western birds as bushtit, verdin, black phoebe, scrub jay, black-throated sparrow, cactus wren, pyrrhuloxia, and brown towhee. Groove-billed ani, vermillion flycatcher, and many other songbirds are present during migration and in the summer. Watch for raptors soaring along the cliffs and fish darting from the shallow waters.

Viewing Information: Probability of viewing featured species is moderate to high. Avoid summer weekends when the park is very crowded. Reservations are recommended.

Directions: *From Uvalde on U.S. 90, drive north on U.S. 83 to Concan and eight miles north to PR 29, which leads to park entrance.*

Ownership: TPWD (512-232-6132)
Size: 1,420 acres
Closest Town: Concan

With its patchwork of open land and forests, an abundance of oaks, and plenty of water, Hill Country is prime white-tailed deer country. "White tails" are a favorite species for wildlife viewing and photography. STEVE BENTSEN

Description: Featuring beautiful wildlands, spectacular bat flights, and cave swallows, this site also harbors a population of the endangered black-capped vireo. Other wildlife includes coyotes, ringtails, raccoons, white-tailed deer, black-tailed jackrabbits, fox and rock squirrels, roadrunners, many songbirds, and a variety of snakes. Red-tailed hawks and other raptors are sometimes observed snagging bats in mid-air. Mexican pinyon pine reaches the eastern limits of its distribution at this site.

Viewing Information: Predictable bat flights occur from April into October. Viewing probability is high for other featured species, except coyote and ringtail, which may be seen at night while leaving the site. Vireos are present only from March to August. Nearby Devil's Sinkhole State Natural Area boasts an even larger bat flight. Both sites can be visited only through reservations or planned tours, and Texas Conservation Passports are required.

Directions: From Brackettville on U.S. 90, go north for twenty-two miles on FM 674 to park entrance.

Ownership: TPWD (512-563-2342)
Size: 6,400 acres   **Closest Town:** Brackettville

Recognized as a good omen by many North American Indians, and the subject of much folklore throughout the Southwest, the roadrunner is also one of our most interesting animals to watch. Its K-shaped tracks are easily identified and will occaisionally lead to where the bird captured a lizard or snake. JEFF FOOTT

100 DEVIL'S RIVER STATE NATURAL AREA

Description: A beautiful biological paradise protecting unique and diverse fauna composed of eastern, western, and tropical species. Many species of fish, including the endangered Devil's River minnow and Conchos pupfish, occur in springs and the river. A surprising number of snakes and lizard species are recorded, the most common being Merriam's canyon lizard and Texas earless lizard. In addition to those species of birds and mammals listed for Garner State Park, look and listen for black-capped vireo and elf owl in the summer. At dusk, watch for bats as they pursue insects. Flower diversity is high.

Viewing Information: Reservations and a Texas Conservation Passport are required and visitation is through guided tours. Fish are easy to see but difficult to identify. Probability is moderate to high for viewing featured land species.

Directions: Call telephone number below for tour reservations and directions.

Ownership: TPWD (512-395-2133)
Size: 20,000 acres   **Closest Town:** Comstock

101 CHANDLER INDEPENDENCE CREEK PRESERVE

Description: Splendid example of Pecos River wilderness and wildlife. Independence Creek, one of only a few perennial streams in west Texas, is home to seventeen species of fish, including the rare proserpine shiner. White-tailed deer, wild turkey, shorebirds, and songbirds can be observed; also the endangered black-capped vireo and many migrating warblers. Coyote, gray fox, bobcat, golden eagle, osprey, and great horned owl are occasionally viewed.

Viewing Information: Probability is high for viewing deer, turkey, and shorebirds in early spring and mid-summer and warblers during spring and fall migration. The probability of observing owls, gray fox, and coyotes is moderate at night and low for other species. Many of the fish can be seen but species identification is difficult. Avoid trespassing on private lands that surround the road into ranch. Visits must be guided by site manager and arranged in advance.

Directions: From Interstate 10, take Texas 349/U.S. 290 exit south to Sheffield, then Texas 349 south about twenty-three miles to dirt road leading to Chandler Ranch. Drive for about six miles to ranch headquarters.

Ownership: PVT (Texas Nature Conservancy, 915-336-7615)
Size: 701 acres
Closest Town: Sheffield

Description: Known for its Native Anerican pictographs and spectacular scenery, this park also is a good spot to view wildlife. During guided tours into the canyon and on the hiking trail along the rim, look and listen for Harris' and other hawks, Chihuahuan and common ravens, black and turkey vultures, canyon and rock wrens, other songbirds, deer, javelina, coyote, ringtail, badger, and four species of ground squirrels. Snakes and lizards can be abundant.

Viewing Information: Viewing probability is moderate to high for all but the javelina and carnivores, which are active at night. Viewing is best very early or late in day.

Directions: *About forty miles west of Del Rio on U.S. 90.*

Ownership: TPWD (512-292-4464)
Size: 2,173 acres
Closest Town: Comstock

Truly a bird of the Southwest, the cactus wren is found at low elevations where cactus, mesquite, and other thorny shrubs are abundant. Its song, which resembles the sound of a car engine that refuses to start, is characteristic of the desert.

SHERM SPOELSTRA

103 AMISTAD NATIONAL RECREATION AREA

Description: The tremendous biological diversity of this area is a consequence of the lake, created by damming the Rio Grande, in a region where the Chihuahuan desert, southern Texas plains, and Hill Country all converge. White-tailed deer, javelina, skunks, jackrabbit, cottontail, wild turkey, wading birds, abundant waterfowl, osprey, golden eagle, Harris' hawk, merlin, black-shouldered kite, numerous shorebirds, three kingfishers, and many songbirds such as Say's phoebe, black-tailed gnatcatcher, olive sparrow, and lark bunting are present. Snakes and lizards are abundant during warm months.

Viewing Information: All of the mammals, except javelina, are likely viewed as are wild turkey, waterfowl during the winter, and many songbirds. Most of the raptors are uncommon and migratory but some, like the American kestrel, are present all year. Wildlife can be viewed along roads leading to, as well as within, the recreation areas like San Pedro Flats and Rough Canyon. The dam and overview area should be visited to observe falcons, eagles, and kingfishers.

Directions: Detailed maps can be obtained at headquarters, two miles northwest of Del Rio on U.S. 90. Go three more miles northwest on U.S. 90 to Spur 454 and San Pedro Flats, then five more miles to Spur 349 and the dam, which is about three miles south. Rough Canyon is 13.6 miles north of headquarters on U.S. 277, then 7.5 miles west on RR 2.

Ownership: NPS, International Boundary and Water Commission (NPS, 512-775-7491)
Size: 67,000 acres   **Closest Town:** Del Rio

The gray fox is fairly common in woodlands throughout Texas, where it is most often seen at dusk or during the night. This fox is skilled at climbing trees and has been found in dens up to thirty feet above ground. Gray foxes eat tremendous numbers of rodents each year. LORRI L. FRANZ

REGION 9: LOWER RIO GRANDE VALLEY AND PLAINS

Tropical species such as the ocelot, green jay, and giant toad reach the northern limit of their ranges in this region, which is characterized by thorny woodlands on the plains and scattered patches of palms and subtropical woodlands in the Rio Grande Valley. These plains were once covered with open grasslands and a scattering of trees, and the valley woodlands were much more extensive. Livestock grazing and agriculture have significantly altered the native range and continue to be the principal land uses. Elevations vary from sea level to 1,000 feet; rainfall averages between eighteen and thirty inches per year.

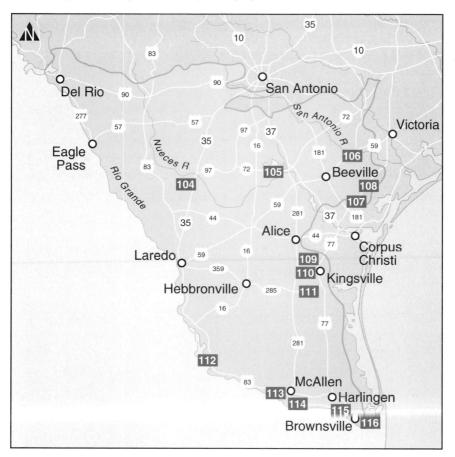

104	Chaparral Wildlife Management Area	**111**	Hawk Alley
105	Choke Canyon State Park	**112**	Falcon Lake/Falcon State Park
106	Goliad State Historical Park	**113**	Bentsen-Rio Grande State Park
107	Welder Wildlife Refuge	**114**	Santa Ana National Wildlife
108	Fennessey Ranch		Refuge
109	King Ranch	**115**	Resaca de la Palma State Park
110	Kingsville Area	**116**	Sabal Palm Grove Sanctuary

104 CHAPARRAL WILDLIFE MANAGEMENT AREA

Description: An exceptionally good reptile viewing area and excellent example of Texas brush country, this site also has recorded more than 180 species of birds. Three endangered reptiles—Texas tortoise, Texas horned lizard, and Texas indigo snake—can be viewed, along with at least twenty-four other reptiles. As many as eleven migratory warblers, twelve sparrows, and six owls occur here. Look for raptors around water tanks where wildlife congregate. White-tailed deer, javelina, feral hogs, coyote, gray fox, striped skunk, badger, bobcat, black-tailed jackrabbit, and eastern cottontail can also be observed.

Viewing Information: Viewing probability is moderate to high for most featured species and low for bobcat, fox, badger, and indigo snakes. An extensive network of roads and a driving tour provide varied viewing. Hike cross-country with care—rattlesnakes are abundant. Wildlife viewing may be discouraged during the hunting seasons. A Texas Conservation Passport and registration at headquarters are required.

Directions: *From Artesia Wells on Interstate 35, take FM 133 west eight miles to headquarters.*

Ownership: TPWD (512-676-3413)
Size: 15,200 acres
Closest Town: Artesia Wells

The Texas tortoise, on the state's list of threatened species, is found throughout the southern part of the state. Tortoises obtain moisture through a diet that includes the pads, fruit, and flowers of prickly pear cactus. LARRY R. DITTO

105 CHOKE CANYON STATE PARK

Description: Abundant javelina, white-tailed deer, coyote, skunks, raccoons, fox squirrels, ground squirrels, and wild turkey can be viewed in both areas of the park and the adjacent Daugherty Wildlife Management Area. Long-billed and curve-billed thrashers and olive sparrows occur in the upland brushlands. Cave swallows nest in the summer under roofs of shelters. The reservoir and small inland lakes are good for black-bellied tree ducks, other waterfowl, and studies of wildlife tracks. Below the dam, shorebirds and wading birds occupy the marsh and songbirds are common in the woodlands. Crested caracara, common in the spring, is viewed all year.

Viewing Information: Viewing probability is high for mammals, songbirds, and turkey but moderate for other featured species. A Texas Conservation Passport is required for the wildlife management area.

Directions: Take Texas 72 west from Interstate 37 to Three Rivers and continue west about four miles to headquarters of south shore unit and about ten more miles to the Callahan unit. Permission to enter the management area and a map to it can be obtained from park headquarters.

Ownership: Bureau of Reclamation (TPWD, 512-786-3538)
Size: 12,500 acres (all units)
Closest Town: Three Rivers

106 GOLIAD STATE HISTORICAL PARK

Description: This site provides a stimulating introduction to the history and wildlife diversity of this part of Texas. Nature trails acquaint the visitor with upland and river bottomland plants, pass by a turkey vulture roost, and present much of the bird and insect diversity. Walking the trails or driving the park roads at night increases the chances of viewing owls and mammals such as raccoon, gray fox, rabbits, and even an occasional ringtail and bobcat. White-tailed deer can be seen during the day and night.

Viewing Information: Viewing probability is high all year for all but the bobcat, fox, and ringtail, which are less common. The best bird and insect watching is from spring into fall.

Directions: Take U.S. 59 or U.S. 183 to the town of Goliad. The park entrance is just south of town.

Ownership: TPWD (512-645-3405)
Size: 178 acres
Closest Town: Goliad

107 WELDER WILDLIFE REFUGE

Description: This refuge offers excellent viewing of south Texas' biological diversity and scenery, boasting fifty-five species of mammals, fifty-five species of reptiles and amphibians, more than 380 species of birds, and 1,400 species of plants. Wildlife diversity is supported by forests along the Aransas River, oak savannahs, brushland, plains, marshes, ponds, and lakes. White-tailed deer, javelina, bobcat, coyotes, and eastern cottontails are featured mammals. Nesting aquatic birds include both species of whistling-duck, purple gallinule, least grebe, white-faced ibis, and black-necked stilt. Twenty-four species of hawks, forty-one of shorebirds, and over forty species of warblers migrate or nest on the refuge. White-tailed hawk and crested caracara are present all year, and merlins can be abundant during fall migration.

Viewing Information: Viewing probability is high all year for deer and small mammals but low to moderate for bobcat and coyotes. It is high for wading birds and songbirds all year and for hawks, waterfowl, shorebirds, and warblers during migration. Guided tours are available to the public at 3:00 p.m. each Thursday. Group tours at other times must be arranged in advance through the headquarters.

Directions: *Entrance is on U.S. 77 about twenty miles northeast of the intersection of U.S. 77 and Interstate 37. Turn south to headquarters.*

Ownership: Welder Wildlife Refuge (512-364-2643)
Size: 7,800 acres   **Closest Town:** Sinton

Although Texas horned lizards are one of our most popular reptiles, they do not survive well in captivity and should never be removed from the wild. Populations declined in the 1950s and 1960s, most likely due to the use of pesticides to eradicate ants, the horned lizard's preferred food.
WYMAN P. MEINZER

108   FENNESSEY RANCH

Description: Each day from fall into spring, thousands of sandhill cranes, geese, ducks, and wading birds fill the sky above a beautiful inland marsh. White-tailed deer and feral hogs wade here, and over forty species of shore-birds migrate through the region. Many wading birds, like the snowy egret, and some ducks, such as the Mexican mallard and black-bellied whistling duck, nest in the marsh. A masked duck has been sighted here. White-tailed hawks and other raptors are common, while songbirds are abundant in the river woodlands and savannah. Coyote, bobcat, javelina, armadillo, jackrabbit, and other small mammals occur throughout the ranch. Alligators are easily viewed near water.

Viewing Information: Viewing probability is excellent from mid-October into March for waterfowl and cranes and all year for wading birds, raptors, white-tailed deer, and the smaller mammals. Other mammals are more difficult to view. Shorebirds viewing is best in March-April and July-August. Waterfowl flights are most dramatic in the early morning and late afternoon. A lodge is being developed. Daily guided visits, group tours, and extended visits must be reserved through the headquarters.

Directions: *Two miles east of Refugio on FM 774, then 4.6 miles south on FM 2678 to ranch entrance.*

Ownership: PVT (800-926-6395)
Size: 4,000 acres   **Closest Town:** Refugio

109   KING RANCH

Description: This site, one of the largest privately owned ranches in the world, preserves large tracts of quality wildlife habitat. In addition to abundant white-tailed deer, javelina, coyote, armadillo, black-tailed jackrabbit, and wild turkey, typical Texas birds such as crested caracara, golden-fronted and ladder-backed woodpeckers, great kiskadee, green jay, bronzed cowbird, and olive sparrow are viewed. Sandhill cranes flock together in fields during winter.

Viewing Information: Daily bus tours, principally to interpret the history and activities of the ranch, take place each hour and offer possibilities of viewing some of the larger wildlife. Probabilities are much better for viewing a greater diversity of mammals and birds on a two-day tour offered by Victor Emanuel Nature Tours (512-328-5221) in October and February through March.

Directions: *Headquarters are located 2.5 miles west of Kingsville on Texas 141.*

Ownership: PVT (512-592-8055)
Size: 825,000 acres   **Closest Town:** Kingsville

110 KINGSVILLE AREA

Description: Several sites in and around Kingsville offer exceptional bird watching opportunities. Dick Kleberg Park and Texas A&I University are good locations for migrating songbirds, green jay, great kiskadee, woodpeckers, vermilion flycatchers, and black-shouldered kites in winter, hooded orioles nesting in the tall palms of the university, and cave swallows beneath a bridge in the park. Santa Gertrudis Creek Bird Sanctuary provides some of the same species plus marsh birds, other hawks, herons and egrets, three species of nesting swallows, and numerous sparrows

Viewing Information: Viewing probability is high for featured songbirds and hawks during the appropriate time of the year. Contact Kingsville Visitor Center (1-800-333-5032) for information on additional sites.

Directions: *Dick Kleberg Park is at the southeast edge of the city just off U.S. 77. Take FM 1717 from U.S. 77 in Kingsville for one mile east to reach Santa Gertrudis Creek. Take Santa Gertrudis Road west from U.S. 77 to the university.*

Ownership: Parks, Kleberg County, (512-595-8591); university, (512-595-3312)

Size: Various   **Closest Town:** Kingsville

Crested caracara are locally common and fun to watch in the southern part of Texas. A member of the falcon family of raptors, caracara are unusual in that they are scavengers and spend a moderate amount of time on the ground.
JOHN SNYDER

Description: One of the best hawk watching areas in the United States with twenty-six species of raptors reported. Thousands of broad-winged hawks, hundreds of Swainson's hawks and Mississippi kites, plus other raptors can be viewed migrating through in March and April and from late August through mid-October. Numerous white-tailed hawks in pursuit of insects escaping the heat are sometimes abundant near prescribed fires on nearby ranches. Crested caracara, white-tailed hawk, Harris' hawk, and others are attracted to several of the chicken farms near Riviera. Check ponds for rare waterfowl and shorebirds. Trees along the roads are productive for interesting songbirds.

Viewing Information: Viewing probability is high for the featured species during migration. Caracara, white-tailed hawk, Harris' hawk, and others are moderately easy to see all year. Viewing is best along "Hawk Alley" or Texas 285, FM 771, and County Road 2340E. Do not trespass onto the chicken farms or private lands. No facilities at this site.

Directions: "Hawk Alley" is the name given to Texas 285 between Riviera on U.S. 77 and Falfurrias to the west. FM 771 and County Road 2340E go east from Riviera to Laguna Salada.

Ownership: State Department of Transportation (512-855-8281)
Size: Thirty miles   **Closest Town:** Riviera

One of nearly fifty species of birds known as "Texas specialties" because they seldom are found in any other state in the U.S., white-tailed hawks are an uncommon permanent resident of the open country in the south of Texas. LARRY R. DITTO

112 FALCON STATE PARK AND FALCON LAKE

Description: A favorite area for bird watchers due to the combination of abundant southwestern species and many tropical species for which this is the most northwestern outpost. It is one of the best locations to see all three kingfishers. Additional species include crested caracara, Harris' hawk, vermilion flycatcher, pyrrhuloxia, brown and green jay, altamira and Audubon's orioles, and other lower Rio Grande specialties. Listen for the distinctive call of common loons in late winter before they migrate. White-tailed deer, javelina, bobcat, raccoon, and black-tailed jackrabbit are commonly viewed at dusk or at night.

Viewing Information: Most birds seen on the park are desert species. The kingfishers, jays, and orioles are most likely viewed in the area just below and east of the nearby dam. Viewing probability for most of the species is moderate to high. Rattlesnakes are common.

Directions: *The park is twenty-five miles southeast of Zapata or fifteen miles northwest Roma via U.S. 83, FM 2098, and PR 46.*

Ownership: TPWD (512-848-5327)
Size: 573 acres
Closest Town: Roma

Vermillion flycatchers usually occur near water, where they fly from a conspicuous perch to catch insects. Males are particularly impressive when they puff up their feathers and flutter upward during their courtship display.
JOHN SNYDER

Description: Protecting wildlife found in no other region of the United States, this park is one of the most outstanding viewing areas in the country. It also protects a part of the subtropical woodlands and shrublands that once covered much of the lower Rio Grande. Ocelot, jaguarundi, bobcat, coyote, javelina, Texas indigo snake, Texas tortoise, and giant toad are viewable. Exceptional birds are the green jay, numerous owls including the tiny elf owl, groove-billed ani, the plains chachalaca, two woodpeckers, six doves including the red-billed pigeon, common pauraque and two species of nighthawks, and altamira oriole. Butterfly watching is good to great all year. Species listed for the following three sites also occur here.

Viewing Information: The probability of viewing cats is low but their tracks and scat can be seen on the trails. It also is low for the snake and elf owl. Chances are high for the other species. Camping provides an opportunity to ride the roads at night looking for pauraque, owls, javelina, coyote, and others.

Directions: From Mission, west of McAllen, drive west for five miles on U.S. 83. Go west on Loop 374 for 1.5 miles to FM 2062, then south to the park.

Ownership: TPWD (512-585-1107)
Size: 578 acres   **Closest Town:** Mission

A tropical bird with tropical colors, the green jay is found in south Texas and nowhere else in the United States. It is a locally abundant permanent resident. The gray jay of the northern Rockies is the only U.S. jay not seen in Texas.
JEFF FOOTT

114 SANTA ANA NATIONAL WILDLIFE REFUGE

Description: Appropriately referred to as the "Gem of the National Wildlife Refuge System," this refuge protects more wildlife diversity than just about any other in the country. It is also one of the few sub-tropical refuges. All of the species listed for Bentsen-Rio Grande State Park occur here, plus the hook-billed kite, gray hawk, northern jacana, Couch's kingbird, rose-throated becard, clay-colored robin, tropical parula, and Audubon's oriole. Unlike most other areas in the United States, up to twelve of the thirty-six warblers listed for the refuge winter in the region. In addition to excellent wildlife viewing, the "A" trail has three lookouts, including a blind, and is accessible for people in wheel chairs and those with impaired sight.

Viewing Information: Viewing probabilities are the same as those at Bentsen State Park. The chances are low to moderate for viewing most species listed here and some like the gray hawk and clay-colored robin are very rare. During the winter months, a tram ride offers a guided tour of the refuge.

Directions: *Drive east from McAllen on U.S. 83 for six miles, turn south on FM 907 for seven miles, then go east on U.S. 281 for a quarter mile to entrance.*

Ownership: USFWS (512-787-7861)
Size: 2,080 acres   **Closest Town:** Alamo

Santa Ana National Wildlife Refuge is part of a larger refuge system that provides a wildlife corridor along the Rio Grande to protect the exceptional biological diversity of the subtropical landscape. Plain chachalacas, a turkey-like bird, are easily seen and heard, even from the tour bus. STEVE BENTSEN

Description: This wild patch of rare tropical woodlands contains many of the Mexican species of wildlife listed for Bentsen State Park and Santa Ana refuge. Although similar, each site is unique with respect to the relative abundance of plants and animals. Part of this park, which was recently cropland, is being restored to provide additional habitat for native wildlife.

Viewing Information: The site is to be developed as a state park, but currently the trail system is limited to primitive roads. Viewing probabilities are about the same as those at Santa Ana wildlife refuge. Until the park opens, registration at area headquarters and a Texas Conservation Passport are required.

Directions: Drive 6.5 miles west of Brownsville on U.S. 281 to Carmen Avenue, an unimproved gravel road. Turn north on this road for about 2.2 miles to entrance.

Ownership: TPWD (512-383-8982)
Size: 1,100 acres
Closest Town: Brownsville

Buff-bellied hummingbirds are most easily seen in the United States at the Sabal Palm Grove Sanctuary, where many other "Texas specialties" are also found.
LARRY R. DITTO

116 | SABAL PALM GROVE SANCTUARY

Description: Tropical bird sounds, ocelot tracks on the trails, and tall sabal palms give this site, one of the most unique in the United States, a distinctively tropical feel. Thirty-two acres of the 172-acre palm sanctuary are virgin palm forest, the remnant of a type of woodland that was widespread in the valley before being cut to make way for agriculture. These palms are home to many of the same species that occur in the previous three sites in the lower Rio Grande valley. The relative abundances of species differ among the sites. For instance, the Central American speckled racer, one of the rarest reptiles in Texas, and the buff-bellied hummingbird are more commonly viewed here than at the other sites. When the resaca contains water, wading birds and waterfowl, including least grebes, are easily viewed from an observation blind. Green parakeets and red-crowned parrots are occasionally seen here and at other valley sites.

Viewing Information: See Site 115 for viewing probabilities. The sanctuary is open 8:00 a.m. to 5:00 p.m. from Thursday through Monday.

Directions: In Brownsville, drive south to the end of the freeway (U.S. 77 and U.S. 83) and turn east on International Boulevard for .7 mile. Take Southmost Road (FM 1419) for about 5.8 miles to the entrance sign.

Ownership: National Audubon Society (512-541-8034)
Size: 172 acres
Closest Town: Brownsville

This sanctuary looks and feels tropical. Efforts are now underway to restore palm groves, as well as some of the other subtropical habitats in the valley, which historically covered much larger areas. LARRY R. DITTO

REGION 10: GULF ISLANDS, MARSHES, AND PRAIRIES

A diverse region of barrier islands along the coast, salt grass marshes surrounding bays and estuaries, remnant tallgrass prairies, oak parklands or "oak motts" scattered along the coast, and tall woodlands in the river bottomlands. Agriculture and urbanization have contributed to the loss of much of the native habitat, resulting in the endangered status of such animals as Attwater's prairie chickens, whooping cranes, Kemp's Ridley sea turtles, and Houston toads. The level terrain ranges from sea level to 250 feet; annual rainfall varies from twenty-eight to fifty-six inches.

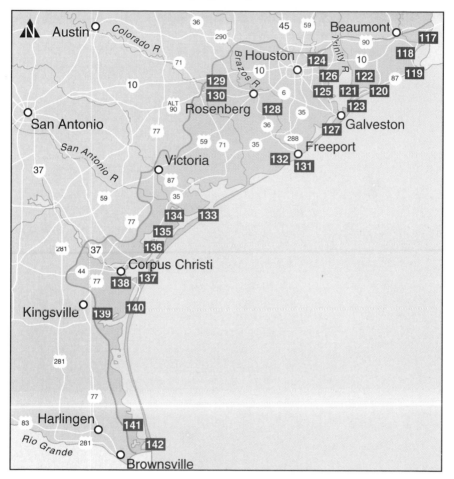

117 Lower Neches Wildlife Management Area	**131** Freeport
118 Murphree Wildlife Management Area	**132** Brazoria National Wildlife Refuge
119 Sea Rim State Park	Complex
120 High Island	**133** Matagorda Island
121 Candy Abshier Wildlife Management Area	**134** Aransas National Wildlife Refuge
122 Anahuac National Wildlife Refuge	**135** Goose Island State Park
123 Bolivar Flats	**136** Rockport/Live Oak Penninsula
124 Sheldon Wildlife Management Area	**137** Mustang Island
125 Armand Bayou Nature Center	**138** Corpus Christi
126 Atkinson Island Wildlife Management Area	**139** Drum Point/Kaufer-Hubert
127 Galveston Island	Memorial County Park
128 Brazos Bend State Park	**140** Padre Island National Seashore
129 Attwater Prairie Chicken National	**141** Laguna Atascosa National Wildlife
Wildlife Refuge	Refuge
130 Eagle Lake	**142** Boca Chica Beach

117 LOWER NECHES WILDLIFE MANAGEMENT AREA

Description: Muskrat are abundant as indicated by their mounds which dot this brackish to freshwater marsh where green-winged teal, northern pintail, and other ducks are found. The area also is home for snow goose, roseate spoonbill and other wading birds, and rails. Shorebirds are abundant and diverse on the tidal flats and alligators are abundant.

Viewing Information: Viewing probability is low for muskrat and black rail. The probability is high for featured waterfowl from late fall through early spring, for wading birds all year, for shorebirds during spring and fall migrations, and for alligators during warm months. Viewing is from the road and system of levees. Wildlife viewing may be discouraged during the hunting season. Registration and a Texas Conservation Passport are required.

Directions: North from Port Arthur on Texas 87 to Bridge City then right on Lake Street for about two miles to where the gravel road enters the management area.

Ownership: TPWD (409-736-2551)
Size: 6,200 acres **Closest Town:** Bridge City

118 MURPHREE WILDLIFE MANAGEMENT AREA

Description: Some of the best habitat for wetland wildlife in the state is found here. The marshes and lakes are rich with diverse waterfowl from October through March. The Lost Lake Unit, a particularly healthy marsh, boasts the largest canvasback duck population in Texas. Anhinga, white-faced ibis, purple gallinule, and common snipes are frequently viewed along with alligators, turtles, and fish. River otter, muskrat, beaver, and nutria inhabit the waters.

Viewing Information: Waterfowl are easily viewed before and after the hunting season. View alligator and gallinule during warm months, snipe during the winter. Nutria are frequently seen; otter, beaver and muskrat are rarely viewed. The chances are high for observing anhingas and wading birds. Registration at area headquarters and a Texas Conservation Passport are required. Wildlife viewing may be discouraged during hunting season. Travel is restricted to boats and boat tours are given periodically.

Directions: Drive on Texas 73 about three miles west of the intersection of Texas 73 and Texas 82 in Port Arthur to headquarters just east of Taylor Bayou. Boats can be launched from bridge over Taylor Bayou and from several sites off of Texas 87 along east side of area.

Ownership: TPWD (409-736-2551)
Size: 13,264 acres **Closest Town:** Port Arthur

Description: A beautiful shoreline for beachcombing, an exceptional boardwalk and nature trail through the salt marsh, and extensive marshlands complete with canoe trails and observation blinds characterize this site. Mink, raccoon, muskrat, rails, least and American bitterns, marsh wrens, boat-tailed grackle, seaside sparrow, alligator, crabs, mosquito fish, and plenty of mosquitos can be seen from the boardwalk. River otter, nutria, white and white-faced ibises, roseate spoonbill and other wading birds, numerous ducks, three species of geese, and alligators are seen in the Marshlands Unit. Gulls, terns, and shorebirds abound on the beach. Thirty-six species of migrating warblers are known from the park.

Viewing Information: Viewing probability is low to moderate for mink and muskrat at night on the boardwalk and low for river otter. Least and American bitterns are common in the summer and winter respectively. Warblers are easily viewed, depending on weather conditions, during spring and fall migrations. Waterfowl are most abundant during the winter, when alligators are least likely to be viewed. Viewing chances are good for other species. The Marshlands Unit is accessible only by boat. Airboats can be chartered for a fee.

Directions: *Take Texas 87 south from Port Arthur to Sabine Pass, then west on 87 for ten miles to park.*

Ownership: TPWD (409-971-2559)
Size: 15,094 acres
Closest Town: Sabine Pass

Wetlands provide habitat for millions of waterfowl and waterbirds, like these purple gallinules, and almost one-third of the nation's threatened and endangered species. Wetlands also supply important nursery and spawning habitat for up to ninety percent of commercial fish catches. Fortunately, there is now a national goal of no overall net loss of wetlands.
LARRY R. DITTO

120 HIGH ISLAND

Description: This site is famous for one of nature's most astounding wildlife spectacles—"fallouts" of migrating songbirds. A fallout typically occurs after a rainy cold front during spring migration. Large numbers of birds representing many species will land in the trees and shrubs along the coast to recover from their flight across the gulf. Birding is good at other times during spring, but numbers are fewer. Twenty to thirty warbler species can be viewed during a day in addition to the scarlet tanager, rose-breasted grosbeak, gray catbird, and others. Warblers include golden-winged, blue-winged, blackpoll, black-throated blue, Cape May, and cerulean.

Viewing Information: Probability of viewing large numbers of birds depends upon the weather. Species composition in the area changes daily and sometimes hourly, which means that the presence of particular species is hard to predict. Please do not stress these birds by harassing them with squeaks or recorded bird songs and do not cross fences or block driveways.

Directions: *Drive south on Texas 124 from Interstate 10 for twenty miles to High Island. Turn east one block at the north end of town, then south a block, then east again to the gate for "Smith Woods" where a small entrance fee is collected. A second grove of trees, "Louis Smith Woods," is on the south end of town about two blocks east of Texas 124 on Fifth Street.*

Ownership: Houston Audubon Society (713-932-1639)
Size: Twenty-five acres
Closest Town: High Island

Many songbirds, like this prothonotary warbler, that migrate from Latin America to the United States to nest are in trouble. Populations are declining; loss of habitat in both breeding and wintering grounds appears to be a major cause. To experience firsthand a landing of these tiny birds after they have flown more than 600 miles across the Gulf of Mexico is to develop a gut-level appreciation of the wonder and fragility of nature.
FREDERICK Q. ATWOOD

Description: This oak grove offers two outstanding wildlife viewing wonders: the "fallout" of migrating songbirds during spring, and the staging of thousands of hawks during their southern migration during the fall. Fallouts are described in the previous site, High Island. Broad-winged, Cooper's, sharp-shinned, and other hawks gather here from flights down the Trinity River and along the coast before continuing south. On good days, hundreds of birds may be viewed during an hour.

Viewing Information: As with High Island, the probability of viewing large numbers of birds depends upon the weather, and the presence of a particular species is hard to predict. Please do not stress the songbirds by harassing them with squeaks or recorded bird songs. A Texas Conservation Passport is required for entry.

Directions: From Interstate 10 at Hankamer, take Texas 61 south to FM 562. Continue south then west on 562 to Smith Point. Follow signs to entrance.

Ownership: TPWD (409-736-2551)
Size: 207 acres   **Closest Town:** Smith Point

Coastal woodlots like this one at Candy Abshier Wildlife Management Area furnish a safe stopover for millions of songbirds to rest and recover from their migration across the Gulf of Mexico. STEPHAN MYERS

122 ANAHUAC NATIONAL WILDLIFE REFUGE

Description: This is one of the best places in the United States to see rails (all nine species occur here) and other marsh birds. Look for black-crowned and yellow-crowned night herons, roseate spoonbill, glossy and white-faced ibises, twenty-two species of ducks, four species of geese, northern harrier and other hawks, and a variety of songbirds. Alligators are common in the waterways. Mammals include bobcat, river otter, muskrat, nutria, and swamp rabbit.

Viewing Information: Viewing probability is highest for waterfowl and raptors from late fall through early spring. It is high all year for rabbits and wading birds. King and clapper rails and common moorhen are easily viewed all year, but the purple gallinule is common only in summer. There is a good chance of seeing bobcat all year, but the chance of viewing aquatic mammals is slim. During spring, songbirds are most diverse in the willows and salt cedars. Warm days bring good chances for viewing alligators. Twelve miles of graveled roads provide excellent viewing but avoid roads during heavy rain. Bring drinking water.

Directions: *South from Interstate 10 on Texas 61 for two miles to FM 562. Continue south on 562 for eight miles, turn east on FM 1985 for four miles to refuge sign.*

Ownership: USFWS (409-267-3337)
Size: 27,506 acres   **Closest Town:** Anahuac

123 BOLIVAR FLATS

Description: Incredible numbers of shorebirds, gulls, and terns are featured here; several rare marine birds have been observed. Herons and egrets are abundant and all three scoter species can be viewed in the surf. Seaside and sharp-tailed sparrows are found in the grass between the highway and beach.

Viewing Information: Migratory shorebird numbers and diversity peak in March and April, then again in July and August as the birds move south. Viewing probability is high for marine birds and moderate for sharp-tailed sparrows in the winter. Other species are easily seen all year. Be careful to avoid disturbing birds at their nests. Wildlife viewing also is good along the beach further east on Bolivar Peninsula. No facilities at this site.

Directions: *Take the free ferry from Galveston to Port Bolivar and go to the north end of town on Texas 87 to where it meets loop 108. Turn east toward the beach then south to Bolivar Flats.*

Ownership: GLO (713-932-1639, Houston Audubon Society)
Size: 550 acres   **Closest Town:** Port Bolivar

Description: Spectacular viewing is provided by large flocks of canvasback ducks and geese during the winter on this freshwater marsh and lake. Numerous other species of ducks, wading birds, and shorebirds can be viewed here. Bald and golden eagles, osprey, and other raptors occupy the area during winter. Raccoons, mink, skunks, nutria, white-tailed deer, and rabbits are present all year as are alligators and bullfrogs.

Viewing Information: Probability is high for watching waterfowl during winter, alligators and bullfrogs during the spring and summer, and wading birds all year. The chances are moderate for bald eagle, raccoon, and skunk. Nutria, deer, and rabbits are easily seen all year. Viewing probability is low for the other species. A Texas Conservation Passport is required for entry. Exercise caution near alligators.

Directions: Take U.S. 90 from Houston northwest to Sheldon, then Sheldon Road north one mile to Garret Road. Turn west on Garret for a little more than two miles to entrance.

Ownership: TPWD (409-736-2551)
Size: 2,503 acres   **Closest Town:** Sheldon

American alligators attract visitors to many wildlife viewing sites, where they are often photographed. Remember, however, that "gators" are wild animals and should never be fed, touched, harassed, or approached too closely. LAURENCE PARENT

125 ARMAND BAYOU NATURE CENTER

Description: Diverse wildlife viewing opportunities characterize this attractive site. From the entrance road, the trails, or the bayou, watch for white-tailed deer and raccoon, laughing gulls and other marine birds, ruddy and other ducks, red-shouldered and other hawks, great egret and other wading birds, migrating warblers and many other songbirds, red-eared sliders and alligators, and insects, particularly butterflies.

Viewing Information: Viewing of all featured species and groups is good to excellent. Waterfowl and songbirds are best viewed during winter and spring respectively.

Directions: *Take Interstate 45 south in Houston to Bay Area Boulevard. Drive east six miles on the boulevard to entrance of nature center.*

Ownership: Harris County (713-474-2551)
Size: 1,900 acres **Closest Town:** Pasadena

126 ATKINSON ISLAND

Description: This scenic island is difficult to reach, but attracts marine birds, migrating songbirds, and raptors. Large numbers of ruby-throated hummingbirds stop during September to feed on honeysuckle and trumpet creeper before continuing south. Northern pintail, American widgeon, gadwall, and other waterfowl are present in winter. Wading birds and other colonial waterbirds roost all year. Coyotes, raccoons, and cottontails occur here.

Viewing Information: Accessible only by boat. Registration with TPWD area headquarters and a Texas Conservation Passport are required to visit island. Guided tours are available periodically. Viewing probability is high for featured species and groups.

Directions: *In Trinity Bay, just east of Morgans Point and the Houston Ship Channel.*

Ownership: TPWD (409-736-2551)
Size: 152 acres
Closest Town: Morgans Point

Description: Diverse habitats and easy access make this island a wildlife watcher's delight. The ocean, bays, open ponds, coastal wetlands, oak groves, prairies, beach, and sand dunes all attract birds and other wildlife. The ferry at the north end of the island is an excellent place to view gulls, terns, and occasionally Atlantic bottle-nosed dolphins. A jetty into the Galveston Ship Channel offers views of black skimmer, five or more species of gulls and abundant terns, including least in the summer and black during migration. Common loons and eared and horned grebes occur in the winter. Kempner Park in Galveston is a good place to witness "fallouts" of migrating songbirds in the spring (see Site 120). Sportsman's Road, near West Bay, is a good spot for shorebirds and wading birds, including reddish egrets and roseate spoonbills. Galveston Island State Park features an extensive beach where gulls, terns, and shorebirds abound and an occasional magnificent frigate bird is seen. Across the highway, nature trails and an observation platform allow viewing access to waterfowl and such marsh wildlife as purple gallinule and other rails, seaside and sharp-tailed sparrows, shorebirds, fish, and crabs. Watch ponds and marshes along the road to San Luis Pass; tidal flats near the pass should be examined for marsh and rare marine birds.

Viewing Information: Viewing probability is low for loons and moderate for grebes, the frigate bird, and dolphins. It is high for all other groups and specific species, unless otherwise noted.

Directions: *From Interstate 45 in Galveston, take Texas 87 east to Seawall Boulevard (FM 3005) and FM 3005 to the dead end then south to the jetty. Or continue on Texas 87 east to the ferry. Kempner Park is at Avenue O and 27th to 29th Streets. Go west on FM 3005 about ten miles from town to the state park. Also, take 61st Street from Interstate 45 south to Stewart Road, then west to 8 Mile Road and north to the Sportsman's Road just before West Bay. San Luis Pass is at the southern end of the island.*

Ownership: Various (409-737-1222, TPWD)
Size: Thirty miles
Closest Town: Galveston

Five species of parrots live in south Texas where their raucous flights fascinate thousands of wildlife watchers. It is uncertain, however, whether any of these species represent native populations or individuals that have been released from captivity.

128 ▮ BRAZOS BEND STATE PARK

Description: Alligators, close-up views of abundant wildlife, noticeable habitat diversity, and beautiful scenery are highlights of this exceptional site. This is one of the best places in Texas to see alligators in their habitat—rivers, creeks, marshes, ponds, and lakes. Snakes also are abundant. White-tailed deer, bobcat, raccoon, cottontail and swamp rabbits, and nutria are common as are songbirds, like painted and indigo bunting, red-eyed and white-eyed vireos, and others. Dramatic viewing of a large rookery of wading birds, as well as a beautiful marsh and waterfowl, is possible from a tall observation tower. Although waterfowl are most abundant in winter, black-bellied whistling and wood ducks can easily be seen in summer. Wildflowers are striking in the prairies and other habitats.

Viewing Information: The chances are excellent for viewing the featured species, except for the bobcat, which is uncommon. Do not feed or annoy alligators. They can be watched safely, but certain rules, available from headquarters, must be followed.

Directions: *From Richmond on U.S. 59 southwest of Houston, go south for approximately twenty miles via Crab River Road (FM 2759) and FM 762 to the park.*

Ownership: TPWD (409-553-3243)
Size: 4,897 acres
Closest Town: Damon

Although once endangered, American alligators are no longer threatened with extinction in Texas. Alligators are the largest reptile in North America, growing to sixteen feet in length. They occur across the easten third of the state and most of the way down the coast. JUDD COONEY

Description: This refuge is managed specifically for a remnant population of the endangered Attwater's race of the greater prairie-chicken, which once numbered over a million. The entire population is now less than 500. Large numbers of waterfowl use the marsh and fields during winter. White-tailed hawks, crested caracaras, prairie falcons, roseate spoonbills, and other wading birds also visit the refuge. White-tailed deer and the endangered Houston toad contribute to the diversity of the region. Wildflowers provide a colorful display in the spring.

Viewing Information: Prairie-chickens can be viewed all year but are most visible during the "booming" or mating season, which lasts from December until May. Visitation is controlled during this period. A blind is available for viewing and photography. Call the refuge office to check on viewing probabilities. Other birds and wildlife can be observed along the auto tour loop or one of the nature trails. Avoid wet roads.

Directions: *From Sealy at the junction of Interstate 10 and Texas 36, go southwest ten miles on FM 3013 to main entrance.*

Ownership: USFWS (409-234-3021)
Size: 8,000 acres   **Closest Town:** Eagle Lake

Some American Indian dances are thought to have been inspired by the courtship display of prairie chickens such as the Attwater's prairie chicken shown here. The prairie chicken "booming" or mating season lasts from December until May. Fewer than 500 of this endangered species remain in Texas.

JOHN SNYDER

130 EAGLE LAKE

Description: Famous for the large flocks of geese (three abundant species) that roost here in the winter, this site also provides excellent viewing of other waterfowl, including over twenty species of ducks. Herons, egrets, and roseate spoonbills are commonly viewed, as are white pelican in winter. Look for fulvous whistling ducks in rice fields around town from April to September. Bald eagles winter at this lake.

Viewing Information: Viewing probability is high to moderate for all but bald eagle, which is less common. Look for geese on the county roads around the town of Eagle Lake. Permission from Lower Colorado River Authority is required to enter lake area No facilities at this site.

Directions: *From Interstate 10 take FM 102 for twelve miles south to town, then two more miles to the lake pumping station where signs will indicate viewing sites.*

Ownership: LCRA (409-234-7336)
Size: 1,200 acres
Closest Town: Eagle Lake

131 FREEPORT

Description: On Christmas bird counts, bird watchers frequently see more species of birds in one day here than at any other site in the United States. The highest record is 226 species and over 200 is typical. Habitat diversity leads to species diversity and habitats here range from beaches, marshes, prairies, farmlands, and river bottoms to oak and pine woodlands, ponds, and bays. Birds include loons, grebes, gulls, terns, herons, egrets, waterfowl, shorebirds, raptors, woodpeckers, and songbirds. Songbird watching is particularly impressive following the passage of cold fronts during spring migration.

Viewing Information: Bird watching is always good at this locality and viewing probability is high for all groups, except loons, which along with the more common grebes, are best viewed in winter.

Directions: *Take Texas 288 south from Houston to Freeport and Texas 332 to the beach and jetties.*

Ownership: Various (409-265-2505)
Size: Various
Closest Town: Freeport

Description: With beautiful marshland scenery and huge populations of geese, ducks, wading birds, and marsh mammals, these three refuges offer a bright future for wildlife as well as exceptional viewing . Brazoria, San Bernard, and Big Boggy refuges are reasonably close together, share diverse habitat types, and harbor the same kinds of wildlife. More than 400 species of wildlife, including at least 250 birds, use these areas. As many as 100,000 or more geese and 40,000 or more ducks winter here. Ten species of wading birds nest here, thirty species of warblers migrate through, and thirteen kinds of sparrows winter here. Mammals found on these refuges include bobcat, coyote, raccoon, armadillo, and river otter. Alligators are common.

Viewing Information: Waterfowl numbers peak December through January. Wading birds are easily viewed all year. Viewing probability is moderate at night or dusk for most mammals. River otters are rare. Brazoria is open to the public only on the first full weekend of each month or, as with Big Boggy, by special arrangements for groups. San Bernard is open during daylight hours. There are no facilities at Big Boggy.

Directions: To reach the San Bernard refuge, go south on FM 2004 from Lake Jackson to Texas 36 where FM 2004 turns into FM 2611. Continue south on FM 2611 for four miles then turn south on FM 2918 for one mile. Turn southwest for two miles on County Road 306 (gravel), then turn south to the entrance. Brazoria refuge is reached by taking Texas 332 from Lake Jackson south to FM 523 and turning north on 523 for about five miles to County Road 227. Turn east on 227 and drive 1.7 miles to the gate, then turn southeast to the entrance. To get to Big Boggy Refuge from U.S. 59, take Texas 60 south from Wharton for thirty-five miles to Wadsworth, turn east on FM 521 for three miles, then south on Chinquapin Road for seven miles to entrance.

Ownership: USFWS (409-849-6062)
Size: 24,455 acres, San Bernard; 40,854 acres, Brazoria; 4,127 acres, Big Boggy
Closest Town: Lake Jackson

Texas is famous for its armadillos, a mammal whose name means "little armored one," referring to its scaly shell. These Texas newcomers arrived here around 1880. They eat beetles, grasshoppers, and centipedes, bear four genetically-identical young of the same sex, and can cross streams by walking on the bottom.

JEFF FOOTT

133 MATAGORDA ISLAND

Description: A wonderful place for beachcombers and bird watchers, this barrier island also is a safe haven for nineteen threatened or endangered species. During the winter, whooping cranes are present in the bayside marshes, while peregrine falcons and piping plovers are found along the coastline. Other threatened and endangered species include the brown pelican, white-faced ibis, reddish egret, white-tailed hawk, woodstork, four species of sea turtles, American alligator, and horned lizard. More than 300 bird species have been recorded for the island, including numerous species of gulls, terns, waterfowl, wading birds, and a variety of songbirds including the seaside sparrow. The island is an excellent place to view shorebirds; up to thirty-seven species gather here by the thousands during migration. Songbird migrations can be equally dramatic. The fascinating flying methods of magnificent frigatebirds, black skimmers, and black-shouldered kites are entertaining to watch. During winter, look for sandhill crane, northern harrier, and short-eared and burrowing owls on the interior grasslands. Tracks in the sand provide evidence of raccoon, badger, coyote, black-tailed jackrabbit, opossum, and feral hogs. White-tailed deer are frequently seen. Be alert for Atlantic bottle-nosed dolphins while riding the ferry to the island.

Viewing Information: Viewing probability is high for shorebirds and songbirds, especially from March to May and again from July to October. Whoopers are best seen from the shuttle during winter. Viewing chances are slim for whoopers and peregrines. The probability is high most of the year for mammals (at least their signs), brown pelican, black-shouldered kite, and skimmer. During the summer, it is high for the frigate bird and moderate for the horned lizard. The Texas Parks and Wildlife Department manages the Matagorda Island State Park. The U.S. Fish and Wildlife Service owns most of the island and manages the Matagorda Unit of the Aransas National Wildlife Refuge. The tidelands are owned by the Texas General Land Office. This island has no telephone service, food, or drinking water, and private vehicles are not permitted. Guided tours are available to holders of Texas Conservation Passports.

Directions: *Take Texas 185 south from Victoria to Port O'Connor. All visitor access is by chartered or private boat, or a ferry that transports visitors the eight miles from Port O'Connor to the island every weekend and during holidays. Visitors can take a shuttle from the dock to the beach.*

Ownership: USFWS, GLO (512-983-2215, TPWD)
Size: 55,393 acres
Closest Town: Port O'Connor

Description: This national treasure is famous as the winter home of the endangered whooping crane, one of the most magnificent birds of North America. Only about 140 remain in the wild today, and over half of these occur on the refuge. This site also boasts over 800 species of plants and almost 500 land vertebrate species, including about 390 species of birds. White-tailed deer, waterfowl, wading birds, shorebirds, songbirds, and frogs are abundant. Alligator, western cottonmouth and other snakes, bobcat, and javelina are relatively common. Wind-shaped live oak trees, abundant wildflowers, open grasslands, and coastal communities support the exceptional wildlife diversity of this refuge and provide outstanding photographic opportunities.

Viewing Information: Most of the wildlife can be seen and photographed from the sixteen-mile auto tour loop and trails. Bobcat and javelina are most likely seen very early or late in the day. Whooping cranes use the grassy salt flats on the southeastern portion of the refuge where the viewing probability is high from November through March. These majestic birds can be watched, usually at a distance, from an observation tower on the refuge or from boat tours originating from nearby Rockport. Alligators and wading birds are easily seen along Heron Flats Trail. Songbird watching is good throughout the refuge but live oak groves are especially productive from mid-March through May when songbirds migrate. Waterfowl are observed during winter from San Antonio Bay and from the Jones Lake viewing platform, which also is a good place to see green tree frogs during warm seasons. For your safety and to protect wildlife habitats, please stay on the trails or in your car. Alligators can be dangerous and no attempt should be made to touch, harass, or feed the animals. An excellent visitor center and interpretive signs aid the viewing experience.

Directions: From U.S. 77, take either Texas 239 or FM 774 to Austwell. One mile south of Austwell, take FM 2040 for seven miles to refuge headquarters.

Ownership: USFWS (512-286-3559)
Size: 54,829 acres   **Closest Town:** Austwell

Recovery of the American alligator population is one of the success stories of the Endangered Species Act. These reptiles, which were almost hunted to extinction, were placed on the list of protected species in 1967. Today, about 150,000 alligators thrive in the wetlands of this state where it is no longer listed as endangered.

Whooping cranes are one of the most magnificent birds in the world. They are also one of the most endangered, with only about 140 left in the wild. To view these cranes is to simultaneously feel awe and reverence for such a beautiful creature, as well as concern for its future. JEFF FOOTT

Cranes are usually seen from boats out of nearby Rockport. The best place at Aransas National Wildlife Refuge (previous page) for viewing cranes is the observation tower shown here, which also provides spectacular views of the coastal salt marsh. About 390 bird species have been observed at this internation- 150 *ally-renowned wildlife refuge.* LAURENCE PARENT

135 GOOSE ISLAND STATE PARK

Description: This small park offers many of the bird watching opportunities and habitats found at Aransas National Wildlife Refuge and Rockport. The ponds, marshes, and shores of the surrounding bays are especially good for shorebirds, rails, and other wading birds. Look for alligators in some of the ponds. Whooping cranes can occasionally be viewed from the park. The national co-champion live oak, "Big Tree," in the northern section of the park is well worth a visit.

Viewing Information: Viewing probabilities are similar to those given for Aransas and Rockport, except for cranes, which are rarely seen at this park.

Directions: Drive ten miles north of Rockport on Texas 35 to PR 13, then two miles east to park entrance.

Ownership: TPWD (512-729-2858) **Size:** 314 acres   **Closest Town:** Fulton

136 ROCKPORT AND LIVE OAK PENINSULA

Description: A bird watcher's heaven, with all groups of birds well represented at least part of the year. Songbirds include veery, gray-cheeked thrush, and many warblers in groves of large live oaks during spring migration. Shorebirds, terns, and gulls are common along coastline. Wading birds are abundant all year. From October to March, waterfowl are numerous and the long-billed curlew and marbled godwit can be seen. Sandhill cranes feed in cultivated fields around the area and endangered whooping cranes can be viewed in the bays from boat tours. Other water birds and Atlantic bottle-nosed dolphins are commonly seen on these tours.

Viewing Information: Birding is great from fall to spring, good in the summer. Details for species, localities, and crane viewing tours are found in a booklet available from the Rockport-Fulton Chamber of Commerce (800-242-0071 in Texas). Tours of islands in the National Audubon Society Sanctuary can be arranged through the sanctuary manager (512-643-3488). There is a Hummingbird Celebration held each September. Drive the Fulton Beach Road and FM 1781 at the east end of the peninsula, plus FM 881 to the northwest, for other viewing opportunities.

Directions: Located thirty-two miles northeast of Corpus Christi on Texas 35.

Ownership: Rockport and various others (512-729-6445)
Size: About four miles by eight miles
Closest Town: Rockport

13 MUSTANG ISLAND

Description: Diverse and accessible habitats, coupled with a mild winter climate create diverse bird watching opportunities at this barrier island. The Port Aransas Ferry is a good place to see Atlantic bottle-nosed dolphin, brown pelican, double-crested cormorant, laughing and ring-billed gulls, and three or more species of terns. Robert's Park, adjacent to the ship channel, is another good site for viewing dolphins and the other species. Dolphins can occasionally be seen in the gulf from Mustang Island State Park, also an excellent viewing area for shorebirds and other water birds. Colonies of water birds can be viewed as they roost on Shamrock Island. Many of these same birds, along with fish and marine invertebrates, are observed at Wilson's Cut. Woody vegetation in the state park and in Port Aransas attracts migrating songbirds by the thousands from mid-March to mid-May, especially following the passage of a cold front into the gulf. Tracks of rabbits, skunks, ground squirrels, and several kinds of wild mice can be found on the dunes.

Viewing Information: Viewing probability is high for all featured species and groups. Brown pelicans are common only in summer while cormorant and ring-billed gull are common only in winter. Shamrock Island, which is private, can be viewed only from a boat. Please do not trespass and do not disturb nesting birds by approaching too closely.

Directions: Take Texas 361 to Port Aransas from either Aransas Pass to the north or from Corpus Christi, via PR 22. After departing ferry at the north end of the island, turn south on Roberts Street and follow signs to Robert's Park. Take PR 53 for fourteen miles south to Mustang Island State Park. Drive 6.5 miles south of Port Aransas airport on PR 53, turn west on shell road for one mile to a canal called Wilson's Cut. Shamrock Island is a mile north of the cut in Corpus Christi Bay.

Ownership: Various (512-749-5246, TPWD)
Size: 3,703 acres (Mustang Island State Park) **Closest Town:** Port Aransas

A common resident along the 624 miles of Texas coastline, the laughing gull attracts and entertains viewers of all ages. Coastal beaches and salt marshes are important feeding grounds for many marine birds and shorebirds.

GEORGE H. H. HUEY

Description: Already a well-known tourist destination, Corpus Christi is becoming famous as a city for watching birds. Numerous sites offer variety in all seasons due to habitat diversity, good climate, and close proximity to the gulf and Mexico. A complete list of these sites appears in a birding brochure available from the visitors bureau. Trees in Blucher Park, in the middle of the city, offer a good spot for songbirds during spring and fall migrations. In Hans A. Suter Wildlife Area, a boardwalk over a marsh on the western shore of Oso Bay provides excellent viewing of wading birds like roseate spoonbill and black-necked stilt, pelicans, ducks, gulls, terns, shorebirds, and songbirds like groove-billed ani. Corpus Christi State University campus is popular because the grassy fields attract long-billed curlews and other shorebirds in migration; the nearby shoreline and open water attract gulls, terns, grebes, scaup, and other waterfowl; the bushes attract songbirds. Ground squirrels are common in the fields. Hummingbirds and butterflies are viewed as they forage on the flowers of plants at the Corpus Christi Botanical Gardens. The walking trail, ponds, and creek here attract a variety of other birds and additional wildlife. A viewing platform is being developed to watch the diverse waterfowl, wading birds, and shorebirds at Red-head Pond.

Viewing Information: Viewing probability is high for the featured species and groups. Waterfowl are most abundant during the winter while shorebird viewing is best in March-April and July-August. A Texas Conservation Passport is required to visit Red-head Pond.

Directions: The entrance to Blucher Park is downtown three blocks south of the courthouse on the 100 block of Carrizo Street. Take Ennis Joslin Road north from Padre Island Drive (Texas 358) along the west side of Oso Bay to the intersection with Niles Drive where Hans Suter Wildlife Area is located. Continue north to Ocean Drive and turn east along the bay to the university campus. To reach the botanical gardens from Padre Island Drive, take Staples Street (FM 2244) south to Oso Creek and look for well-marked entrance. Red-head Pond is two miles southwest of Padre Island Drive on Waldron Road, then .5 mile south on Glen Oak Drive.

Ownership: City of Corpus Christi and others (800-678-OCEAN, Visitors' Bureau)
Size: Various
Closest Town: Corpus Christi

139 DRUM POINT AND KAUFER-HUBERT MEMORIAL COUNTY PARK

Description: Most of the wading birds in Texas, including white-phase reddish egrets, white pelican, and roseate spoonbill, can be viewed all year at these sites. They also harbor abundant waterfowl in the winter, including both species of scaup and two of scoter. Shorebirds on the extensive mudflats are particularly abundant and diverse during spring and summer migration. Black skimmer, black-necked stilt, Wilson's plover, and least terns nest here. Swallows migrate in vast numbers in April and September, with all North American species represented except the violet-green. Look for migrating raptors in abundance from March to April and late August to mid-October.

Viewing Information: Viewing probability for the featured groups is high during specified seasons as it is for many species within each group.

Directions: Eleven miles south of Kingsville on U.S. 77, go east on FM 628 for six miles, then north on County Road 1120 for two miles. Take County Road 2250 east two miles, then County Road 1132 north to the bluff and continue on unimproved road to shoreline and point. To reach the park, continue on FM 628 east past County Road 2250 for about two miles as it turns southeast through Loyola Beach to the park.

Ownership: Kleberg County (512-595-3312)
Size: 100-plus acres
Closest Town: Riviera

The long-billed curlew is the largest of the thirty-three species of shorebirds seen in Texas, and has the longest bill, which enables the curlew to probe for food beneath the sand. The wild call, a clear, mellow whistle that sounds like cur-lee, cur-lee, *is thrilling to wildlife watchers.* GEORGE H. H. HUEY

Description: One of the most picturesque, unspoiled, and biologically diverse islands along the southern coast of the United States. Although best known for its recreational opportunities, the national seashore also is one of the best places for viewing wildlife. Beaches, dunes, grasslands, ponds, marshes, and tidal flats are constantly being changed by wind, rain, and storms. As on other barrier islands, wildlife viewing opportunities vary remarkably as bird migrations ebb and flow. Waves of shorebirds and warblers in the spring and fall bring new surprises for both amateur and experienced bird watchers. There are thirty-eight species of shorebirds and thirty-two species of warblers recorded for the area. The island also is known for the migrations of peregrine falcons that peak in late September and early October. Ghost crabs scurrying to their holes in the sand, laughing gulls swirling overhead, and sandpipers skittering in front of the waves entertain kids young and old. Bird Island Basin is an excellent place to see white pelican, reddish egrets and other wading birds, and waterfowl. The grasslands are home to meadowlarks, killdeer, sandhill cranes from fall to spring, and the Padre Island kangaroo rat, an attractive mammal found nowhere else on earth. Coyotes, ground squirrels, gophers, and jackrabbits also are common. With Atlantic bottle-nosed and Atlantic spotted dolphins common in the gulf near the beach and five species of rare sea turtles, all threatened or endangered, this island offers the best chance in Texas of seeing marine wildlife from shore. It also is a joy just to watch the abundant sea oats in motion with the sea breezes.

Viewing Information: Probability of viewing featured species, except turtles, is high all year, except where seasons are given. Chances of observing turtles are low. Although the kangaroo rat may not be seen very often, its foot and tail tracks can be seen in the sand along the Grasslands Nature Trail. Hiking across the dunes is prohibited. The seashore is more than eighty miles long, but only the northern fourteen miles can be driven without a four-wheel drive vehicle.

Directions: *From Corpus Christi, drive southeast on Padre Island Drive (Texas 358) to PR 22. Cross the causeway and continue south on PR 22 for about thirteen miles to the entrance.*

Ownership: NPS (512-937-2621)
Size: 133,918 acres   **Closest Town:** Corpus Christi

Padre Island (previous page) is a perfect place for sunsets and beachcombing. This national seashore is large enough for a person to find a place to stand alone at the edge of the sea and contemplate our changing life on earth. GEORGE H. H. HUEY

Padre Island (previous page) is home to crabs on the beach, dolphins in the gulf, wading birds in the bay, and peregrine falcons slicing through the air. These magnificent predators are most often seen during the peak of fall migration.
STEVE BENTSEN

Description: The exciting possibility of viewing an ocelot is better in the wildlands here than at any other place in the United States, but even here the chances are very slim. The rare jaguarundi, uncommon mountain lion, and common bobcat, also inhabit this refuge. White-tailed deer are common. This is one of the best bird watching sites in the United States with 392 species of birds, including thousands of waterfowl in the winter, thousands of shorebirds and songbirds during spring and fall migrations, and resident Mexican specialties like the chachalaca, great kiskadee, green jay, and Couch's kingbird. Harris' and white-tailed hawks nest here and can occasionally be viewed. Butterflies, lizards, and snakes are abundant most of the year because the climate is so mild. Two self-guided auto tours, several hiking trails, and an observation area provide a variety of excellent viewing opportunities.

Viewing Information: Whereas the viewing probability is low for the cats, their tracks and scat can be found on the trails. Viewing chances are moderate for the hawks, kingbird, jay, and kiskadee. The other species and groups are easily viewed.

Directions: From Harlingen, travel about twenty-five miles east on FM 106 to Buena Vista Road, then north on Buena Vista for three miles to refuge headquarters.

Ownership: USFWS (512-748-3607)
Size: 45,187 acres   **Closest Town:** Rio Hondo

Less than 120 ocelots remain in Texas. These cats depend on extremely dense brush for survival, a habitat that has been reduced to about five percent of what once occurred in the Rio Grande Valley and coast. The habitat type, small population, and nocturnal habits make ocelots very difficult to view.
ERWIN AND PEGGY BAUER

142 BOCA CHICA BEACH

Description: Large tidal flats, tall sand dunes, miles of open beach, beautiful surf, and marshes characterize this site. Shorebirds can be spectacular during migration, which usually peaks in April and late July. Gulls, terns, and wading birds also are abundant and diverse, including occasional rarities. Late September is a good time to watch the fall migration of falcons.

Viewing Information: Viewing is from the road to the beach, then south on the beach to the Rio Grande. North of Texas 4 and to the west is South Bay, which is a coastal preserve with abundant wildlife watching opportunities. Viewing probability is high during stated seasons.

Directions: *Take Texas 4 east from Brownsville about twenty-five miles to beach.*

Ownership: GLO (512-541-8034)
Size: Seven miles   **Closest Town:** Brownsville

One of the best kept secrets of Texas, Boca Chica Beach and surrounding areas offer beauty, solitude, diverse and extensive coastal habitats, and abundant wildlife depending on the season. STEVE BENTSEN

WILDLIFE INDEX

Index to the sites where particular wildlife groups and selected species are most likely observed. Species and species groups are listed alphabetically.

MAMMALS

Bats: 78-79, 84, 91, 94, 99

Carnivores: Black bear 69, 77-79 Bobcat 6, 10, 77, 134, and others, Foxes 65, 93, 95, 100, and others Mountain lion 69, 78-79 Ocelot 113-116, 141

Freshwater mammals: 6, 13, 16, 40, 56, 60, 78, 117-119, 132

Hoofed mammal: Bison 21, 93 Collared peccary (javelina) 77-79, 105, 107-109 Elk 69 Mule deer 3, 10-11, 65, 69, 73-74, 78-79 Pronghorn (antelope) 1, 68, 75 White-tailed deer 19, 41, 78, 82-84, 88-93, 97, 134, and others

Marine mammals: 127, 133, 136-137, 14U

Small mammals: Armadillo 32, 44-45, 61-62, 93, 132, and others Chipmunk 69 Porcupine 3, 10-11, 69 Prairie dog 1, 3, 15, 68

BIRDS

Hummingbirds: 35, 65, 69, 78-79, 113-116, 134, 136, 138, 141

Marine birds: 119, 123, 126-127, 131, 133, 135-140, 142

Parrots: 113-116

Raptors: Caracara 105, 107-109, 111-112, Eagles 10, 41, 67, 69, 73, 78, 81 Hawks 1, 10, 31-32, 65, 67, 73, 77-79, 107-109, 111, 121, and others Kites 6-7, 111, 113-116, Osprey 22, 34, 43, 81, 103 Owls 1, 15, 31, 100 Peregrine falcon 69, 78, 133, 140, 142

Shorebirds: 123, 126, 131, 133, 135-137, 139-142

Songbirds: Black-capped vireo 23, 83-84, 9S-96, 99 Bluebirds 10-11, 39, 69, 74 Buntings 21, 44, 61, 128 Golden-cheeked warbler 83-85, 88, 92, 96-97 Green jay 112-116, 141 Other Warblers 43-45, 58-61, 78, 113-114, 116, 119-121, and others

Upland birds: Chachalaca 113-116, 141 Prairie chickens 6, 129 Quail 12, 31, 38, 65, 73-74, 76 Wild Turkey 6, 9, 90, 93, 101

Wading birds: 16, 34, 52, 103, 108, 118, 123, 126, 128 and others Sandhill crane 4, 5, 108, 109, 140 Whooping crane 133-136

Waterfowl: 2, 5, 8, 16, 30, 34, 40, 108, 118, 122, 124, 130, 132, and others

Woodpeckers: Red-cockaded 48-51, 53, 57, 61, 63 Pileated 43, 50, 58, 61,

REPTILES/AMPHIBIANS

15, 25, 61, 65, 76-79, 104, 116, 134 and others American Alligator 40, 119, 122, 124, 128, 134, Giant toad 113-116 Horned lizard 77-79, 104, 133 Houston toad 43, 129 "Red racer" 77-79, Texas tortoise 104, 111-116, 141

FISH

36, 71-72, 78, 82, 85-88, 96, 100-101

INSECTS

Butterflies 35, 78-79, 84, 113-116, 125

WILDFLOWERS

1, 18, 23, 32, 35, 38, 61, 78, 96, 128, and others